ASTOUNDING SACRIFICE

The Most Crucial Event in All of Human History

John G. Hutchinson

ISBN: 978-1-77069-653-2

Printed in Canada

Word Alive Press
131 Cordite Road, Winnipeg, MB R3W 1S1
www.wordalivepress.ca

WORD ALIVE PRESS
Just Write!

MIX
Paper from
responsible sources
FSC
www.fsc.org   FSC® C016245

Library and Archives Canada Cataloguing in Publication

Hutchinson, John G., 1932-
    Astounding sacrifice : the most crucial event in all of human history / John G. Hutchinson.

ISBN 978-1-77069-653-2

    1. Jesus Christ--Passion. 2. Jesus Christ--Resurrection.
3. Jesus Christ--Ascension. 4. Suffering of God. I. Title.

BT400.H88 2012   232.4   C2012-903836-9

ENDORSEMENTS

This book comes at a critical moment in Church history. Not only have we entered the age of deception in society—it is also to be found at many levels within the Church itself!

In this book, John Hutchinson has given us a timely plumb line! Without the focus on the cross and the events leading up to the crucifixion and the resurrection and the ascension—as well as Pentecost—we have a Christianity without any substance!

However, the contents of this book enable us to refocus on the profound gift God has made available to us in Christ. With the focus of the power of the cross in place—it explains what the real Father-heart of God means—it explains the place of the miraculous and supernatural in a day and age when many are looking for signs and wonders. It also enables us to understand what the signs of the times really involve and the part we need to play in what must be seen as the most dramatic moment in biblical history.

Every serious Christian needs a copy of this book in order to maintain the plumb line of integrity in our belief and practice as members of the Body of Christ in a day and age when the world is so desperately hungry for truth that is eternal. The Father has given us a gift of inexpressible value—the contents of this book explain why.

Rev. Dr. Alistair P. Petrie
Founder and Executive Director of Partnership Ministries

John Hutchison's book *Astounding Sacrifice* is a magnificent work that will delight anyone who delights in the Bible. *Astounding Sacrifice* integrates into one fascinating and easy-to-read narrative the details of the four Gospels. It provides a deeper and more profound understanding of all that Jesus accomplished for us through His crucifixion, burial, resurrection and ascension. *Astounding Sacrifice* will enlarge your faith. It will release you of doubts about God's love for you. And it will empower you to receive more fully His gifts of amazing grace, unconditional forgiveness and immeasurable love. I highly recommend *Astounding Sacrifice.*

Judy Rushfeldt
Award-winning author, speaker, and online magazine publisher

Astounding Sacrifice is truly a labor of love inspired by the Holy Spirit that clarifies the events of the last few weeks of Christ's life on earth as fully man and fully God.

John Hutchinson has beautifully integrated this authentically biblical account, from the four Gospels, of the crucifixion, resurrection and ascension of Jesus Christ, which is undeniably the most crucial event in all of human history.

John has inserted very helpful information and explanations that are invaluable in further Bible study. This is not only a logical reference and study manual but can be a wonderful devotional reading experience.

Rev. Don Harbridge
Former pastor and Christian bookstore owner

The crucifixion and resurrection of Jesus Christ is without question the single most important event in the history of the world. As a result, Jesus is the only person to have risen from the dead, thereby conquering sin, death, hell, and the wrath of God. Written through an in-depth study of the four Gospel narratives, John Hutchinson provides grounded biblical evidence confirming the historical fact that Jesus died on a cross, was buried in a tomb, and resurrected to give eternal life. From skeptics, atheists, seekers, and searchers to those of the Christian faith, the teaching of this book will be sure to answer your questions and leave you with hope and clarity in your faith journey.

Dwight Van Middlesworth Jr.
University student

DEDICATION

First and foremost, I dedicate this book
to glorify our great Heavenly Father and
His immeasurable Astounding Love for us all,
that compelled Him to plan, prophesy, and accomplish
the Astounding Sacrifice of His dearly beloved Son, Jesus
Christ;

And also to glorify our wonderful Savior,
Jesus, Who is "God manifest in the flesh"
and Who, because of His Astounding Love for us,
embraced the Astounding Sacrifice of His sinless Self,
for our redemption, forgiveness, transformation, and eternal
salvation.

Secondly, I lovingly dedicate this book to
Reta, my dear wife, who was a wonderful,
loving, faithful, supportive, and vivacious partner,
both in our marriage and in our service to Jesus Christ.
God graciously used her to uniquely bless many, many people.

TABLE OF CONTENTS

ACKNOWLEDGMENTS

Much gratitude and credit goes to my dear friend and sister-in-Christ Janice Pasay, who helped me very, very much in getting my previous book, *Astounding Love: Experience God's Immeasurable Father-Love for You,* finished and published. She did a great amount of research for me, on authoring, editing, and publishing, as well as doing a lot of typing and advising.

And now, she again has been a great help in getting this manuscript finished and ready for publishing. Her very valuable assistance is deeply appreciated. God bless and reward you, Janice!

Also, my appreciation goes to my dear longtime friend and brother-in-Christ Rabbi Cal Goldberg, who is the rabbi of Beth Shechinah, a Messianic congregation of Jews and non-Jews who believe that Yeshua (Jesus) is the Messiah.

Quite some time ago, when I was nearly finished integrating, from the four Gospels, this narrative of Jesus' crucifixion, resurrection, and ascension, there were just a few details that I could not quite reconcile. I mentioned this to Rabbi Cal, and immediately he said to me, "Oh, didn't you know that the Pharisees observed the Passover high Sabbath on the fourteenth day of the month Nisan, but the Sadducees observed the Passover high Sabbath one day later, on the fifteenth day of Nisan?"

I replied to Cal that I had never heard this before. When I applied this insight to the integrated narrative, everything fell into place! God bless you, Cal, and Beth Shechinah!

I am also deeply grateful to my family, friends, and colleagues who have taken the time to peruse and critique my manuscript. They have given me good and helpful suggestions, as well as encouragements. God bless you all!

INTRODUCTION

Dear Reader,

The following points are *very important* for you to fully understand and appreciate this book. Please take a few moments to read this introduction, before you begin to read the book.

• This all started for me many years ago, when I began wondering if all the details of the crucifixion and resurrection from the four Gospels could be harmoniously integrated with no contradictions. I finally found that *they could all fit together,* and that it gave *a much more comprehensive understanding* of all that Jesus suffered and accomplished in His crucifixion, burial, resurrection, and ascension. I had no intention of ever publishing it, but recently God has said very clearly to me that it should be shared with many.

• A more complete and a deeper insight into the most crucial event in all of human history is the reason for combining all the details of the four Gospels into *one harmonious narrative.* In integrating these four accounts into one, I have been as diligent as possible, asking God to help me to be accurate and true to the Scriptures and not let any human ideas or speculations enter in. I do not claim that my integration of the four Gospels is inerrant. But it is to me the most likely way that all four accounts fit together in harmony.

- God had His perfect reasons for giving us four separate narratives through four different men, because each of the four Gospels has its own unique theme and target audience. My combining them is *not* to improve on what God has done, but to get *a fuller and richer picture* of, and *a deeper appreciation* for, His Astounding Sacrifice. I believe that each of the Gospels should also be studied separately on its own.

- God is the author of the Scriptures. I am just one whom God has chosen to integrate and compile into this one complete narrative the different accounts of Jesus' crucifixion, burial, resurrection, and ascension, which are recorded in the four Gospels of the New Testament—namely, Matthew, Mark, Luke, and John.

- Every detail recorded in these four Gospels is integrated into this one consecutive, complete story, beginning at the main section entitled "Jesus' Last Passover Supper" and continuing until the end of the main section entitled "Jesus Pours Out the Promise of the Father."

- The portions enclosed in textboxes are not part of the narrative. I am calling them windows, because they will shed light on the narrative. They are inserted for a fuller understanding and personal acceptance of the *most crucial* event in all of human history.

- Words or phrases in square brackets are explanations of words or phrases that may be unfamiliar to some people or are words added to provide understanding or context.

- The first main section, entitled "Jesus—The Astounding Revelation of God, Himself, to Us All" is a paraphrase of various key Scriptures to make very clear Who Jesus really is.

• The second main section, "Jesus Deliberately Prepares for His Death," is just excerpts from that period of Jesus' life, and *not* every detail.

• The subsection entitled "Explanations of the Jewish Feast of Passover and the Different Sabbaths" provides *very important*, and little-known, insights into this narrative.

• The subsections entitled "Why God Sacrificed His Own Beloved Son," "The Astounding Shed Blood of Jesus," "God Raises Jesus from the Dead," and "The Exalted Position of the Ascended Jesus" are paraphrases of and excerpts from key Scriptures to make very clear *the main reasons* for, and the wonderful *purposes and accomplishments* of, Jesus' crucifixion, burial, resurrection, and ascension.

• The subsection entitled "What Exactly Is the Authentic Gospel of Jesus?" describes what Jesus said was necessary for the gospel to be complete. It is very important!

• The sections entitled "Receiving Jesus' Astounding Sacrifice," "Jesus Greatly Desires Everyone to Receive His Astounding Sacrifice," "How to Receive Jesus and His Great Salvation," "A Prayer to Receive Jesus," and "Jesus—God's Astounding Love-Gift Sacrifice, for Us All" are opportunities for *personal acceptance* of the wonderful salvation that our heavenly Father has provided for us, through Jesus.

• This book is based on God's Word, the Holy Scriptures, which we commonly call the Bible. I honor and revere the entire Bible as God's Word and believe that it was given by the inspiration of God, to holy men of God. I believe the many promises that God has given in Scripture that His Word will endure forever and be preserved to every generation. I believe that the Word of God we have today has been supernaturally preserved by God and is *absolutely true*.

- Ordinary, common English is used, and I have earnestly asked God to keep me *true to His Scriptures.*
- Endnotes have been inserted to reference the source Scripture for the text. The endnote number gives the Scripture reference for the preceding words or for the entire portion of the text following the previous endnote.

The Father's Astounding Love for us, His children, compelled Him to make His dearly beloved Son, Jesus, the Astounding Sacrifice, to pay the penalty for all our sin. And it was Jesus' Astounding Love for us that made Him willing to sacrifice His sinless Self for our salvation and our eternal life. In the year 2011, I published a book entitled *Astounding Love: Experience God's Immeasurable Father-Love for You.* In that book, I deal with God's great love more fully. I recommend it to you. For further details and information about ordering copies, please visit: http://www.astoundingfatherlove.com/.

PREFACE

Astounding Sacrifice? Yes, it is absolutely astounding! In fact, "astounding" is an understatement!

I am utterly astonished when I consider how great is the immeasurable love that God has for us humans and that He would make such an incredible sacrifice for people like us, in order to reconcile us back into His loving arms again.

The God Who designed and created the universe—from the tiniest subatomic particles to the vast whirling galaxies—decided to create us, on this tiny planet Earth, as His very own special children, in His likeness and in His image.[1] God then breathed His Spirit and His life into them, making them living souls.[2] Thus, their spirits were originally filled with the Spirit of God.

The Bible makes it abundantly clear that the very core nature of God is love[3]—eternal, unchanging, infinite, unconditional love—full of goodness, mercy, grace, and forgiveness, and also that His love is forever true, faithful, righteous, and totally just.

I believe He created us because His great loving Heart wanted to pour out His abundant love upon a whole bunch of His children and also for them to pour out their love back to Him in joyful, deep gratitude, thus thrilling His loving Heart.

But eventually Adam and Eve disobeyed God and sinned. Therefore God's Spirit had to depart from them, because God is holy and cannot be in union with sin. This left man's spirit empty, cold, lonely—and dead!

But the very day that Adam and Eve sinned, God provided the skins of animals to cover them.[4] This necessitated sacrificing the animals and shedding their blood, which was a prophetic picture of the future sacrifice of Jesus, "the Lamb of God,"[5] shedding His blood for us, thus covering our sin.

From that day onwards until Jesus' crucifixion, God required every person to sacrifice animals for the covering (forgiveness) of their sins. When they did this by faith in obedience to God, He accepted these sacrifices as a covering for their sin until His only Son, Jesus, made the ultimate sacrifice of Himself on the cross for the sins of the whole human race—past, present, and future, thus paying the full penalty for our sin.[6]

God very carefully planned the crucifixion, burial, resurrection, and ascension of Jesus and prophesied many of the details throughout the Old Testament Scriptures, hundreds of years before Jesus came.

Then, in His perfect time, God did a most astounding thing: God's only Son, Jesus, became flesh and lived among us—a real man right down on our level![7] In Jesus dwells all the fullness of God's character and nature—bodily![8]

Jesus, God manifest in the flesh,[9] came to reveal the Father and to teach, preach, and do many miracles. But far more than all that, He came to sacrifice Himself on the cross and in the tomb, to pay the full penalty for the sins of the whole world[10]—including yours and mine—and rise triumphantly from the dead!

God the Father loves us so greatly and desires us so passionately that He sacrificed His only, dearly beloved Son,

Jesus, on that cross for each one of us, so that He could totally forgive us, cleanse us, clothe us with His righteousness, and joyfully accept us back into His great loving Arms.

Now, you can personally receive God's wonderful Holy Spirit into your spirit. He will gladly unite with, and fill, your empty, cold, lonely spirit, forever! This will be "the most crucial event" of your whole life—and for eternity!

Jesus is God's Astounding Sacrifice for us! Absolutely astounding!

The Astounding Sacrifice of Jesus Christ, Son of the Living God

THE MOST *CRUCIAL* EVENT IN *ALL* OF HUMAN HISTORY

A COMPLETE ACCOUNT OF THE
CRUCIFIXION, BURIAL, RESURRECTION, AND *ASCENSION*
OF JESUS CHRIST, THE MESSIAH,
WOVEN TOGETHER FROM THE FOUR GOSPELS
INTO ONE NARRATIVE

CHAPTER ONE

JESUS—THE ASTOUNDING REVELATION OF GOD

I n the beginning God created the heavens and the earth. In the beginning, already existing, was "THE WORD" [Jesus], and the Word was with God, and the Word was God.[11]

All things were created by Him. In Him was the life of God, and His Life was the light of men.[12]

When the right time had come, God sent His Son, born of a woman, to redeem us, that we might be adopted as His children.[13]

THE BIRTH OF JESUS IS ANNOUNCED

God sent His angel Gabriel to a virgin called Mary. Gabriel said to her, "You shall conceive in your womb, and give birth to a Son, and shall call His name JESUS [which means "God saves"]. He shall be great, and shall be called the Son of the Highest. The Holy Spirit shall come upon you, and the power of the Highest shall overshadow you: therefore the Holy One Who shall be born of you shall be called the Son of God."[14]

All this was done to fulfill what the Lord spoke [about 700 years earlier] through the prophet Isaiah; Isaiah said, "A virgin shall become pregnant, and bear a Son, and they shall call His name Immanuel," which is translated as "God with us."[15]

For to us a Child is born, to us a Son is given. The dominion will be upon His shoulder. And His name will be called Wonderful Counselor, Mighty God, Everlasting Father, Prince of Peace.[16]

JESUS—GOD MANIFEST IN HUMAN FLESH

So the Word was made flesh and lived among us, and we saw His glory, the glory of the only Son of the Father, full of grace and truth.[17]

He Who was from the beginning, Whom we have heard, Whom we have seen with our eyes, Whom we have looked upon, and our hands have touched, is the Word of Life. The Life was revealed, and we have seen Him, and we bear witness and show to you the Eternal Life, Who was with the Father. The One we have seen and heard, we declare to you.[18]

Great is the mystery of God-likeness: God was manifest in the flesh.[19] For it pleased the Father that in Jesus, all the fullness of God's nature should dwell bodily.[20]

As mentioned in the Introduction, "windows" like the one following are inserted to shed further light on the narrative.

God named Jesus "The Word" because Jesus is God the Father's communication, declaration, expression, revelation, and demonstration of His Own wonderful character and nature—sent to us in human flesh and blood, right down on our level—because the Father loves and desires us so greatly and so intensely!

It has been pointed out that because it was man who sinned, so it had to be a sinless man who could atone (pay the penalty) for that sin.

The Astounding Humility of God

Although Jesus was equal with God, He laid that aside, took the form of a servant, and was made in the likeness of men. And being found in appearance as a man, He humbled Himself and became obedient to the point of death, even the death of the cross.[21]

The Astounding Reason Why God Sent His Son, Jesus

Jesus was made like us, a little lower than the angels, in order to suffer death. Since we are made of flesh and blood, He Himself also shared in flesh and blood, so that through death He might destroy him who had the power of death—that is, the devil—and deliver us from this present evil world.[22] God demonstrates His astounding love toward us, in that while we were still sinners, Christ died for us.[23]

God so greatly and intensely loved the whole human race that He gave, and sacrificed, His only Son, that whoever believes in Him should not perish but have everlasting life. God did not send His Son into the world to condemn the world, but that the world through His Son, Jesus, might be saved.[24]

From the creation of the world, God the Father planned that Jesus would be slain as the Passover Lamb of God Who takes away the sin of the world.[25]

> *Jesus was born in the town of Bethlehem in the region of Judea and was raised in a lowly family, in the town of Nazareth in the northern region of Galilee, which is now part of the state of Israel. He was brought up to be a carpenter.*

He began His ministry at about thirty years of age, travelling around preaching, teaching, making disciples, performing miracles, healing the sick, casting out demons, and raising the dead.

After about three and one-half years of ministry, He determined to go to Jerusalem one more time. This time, it was to fulfill the greatest purpose of His coming to earth— namely, His crucifixion, resurrection, and ascension.

CHAPTER TWO

JESUS DELIBERATELY PREPARES FOR HIS DEATH

HE REPEATEDLY PREDICTS HIS DEATH

While Jesus was still in Galilee, as He was alone praying, His disciples joined Him. He asked them, "Who do people say that I, the Son of Man, am?" They answered, "Some say John the Baptist, some, Elijah, and others, Jeremiah or one of the prophets."

"But who do you say that I am?" He asked.

Simon Peter answered, "You are the Christ, the Messiah, the Son of the living God."

"Blessed are you, Peter," Jesus responded. "For you did not come to know this on your own, but My Father Who is in heaven has revealed this to you."[26]

> *"Christ" is the Greek word for the Hebrew word "Messiah." The Hebrew word "Messiah" means the promised one, who is commissioned and sent from God to save His people.*

From that time on, Jesus began to teach them that He would go to Jerusalem; suffer many things; be rejected by the elders, chief priests and scribes; be killed; and after three days rise again.[27]

Another time, while they were still in Galilee, Jesus said to His disciples, "Let these sayings sink down into your hearts: the Son of Man shall be betrayed and handed over to men who shall kill Him, and He shall rise again after the third day."

They were very sad, but they did not understand what He said and were afraid to ask Him.

When the time came that He should be received up to heaven, He steadfastly determined to go to Jerusalem.[28]

Jesus went ahead of them when they were on the road going up to Jerusalem. They were amazed at this and, as they followed, they were afraid.

> *The disciples likely were amazed that Jesus was going to Jerusalem because He had told them that He would be killed there. They were likely afraid for the same reason.*

Then He took the twelve disciples aside on the road and began to tell them again the things that would happen to Him, saying, "Look, we are going to Jerusalem, and everything that was written by the [Old Testament] prophets concerning the Son of Man will be fulfilled: the Son of Man will be betrayed and delivered to the chief priests and the scribes, and they will condemn Him to death and take Him to the Gentiles [the Romans]. They will mock Him, whip Him, spit on Him, and crucify Him. And He will rise again after the third day."

But they understood none of this; the meaning of what Jesus said was hidden from them.[29]

HE IS ANOINTED FOR BURIAL

Six days before the Passover, Jesus came to Bethany, where Lazarus lived. Lazarus had been dead, but Jesus had raised him from the dead. There they made Him a supper. Lazarus' sister Martha served, and Lazarus was one of those who sat at the table with Him.

Then Lazarus' other sister, Mary, took a pound of very costly perfumed spikenard oil, anointed the feet of Jesus, and wiped His feet with her hair. The house was filled with the fragrance of the oil.

One of His disciples, Judas Iscariot, Simon's son, who would betray Him, complained, "Why was this oil not sold for three hundred denarii [Roman coins, being about one year's wages] and given to the poor?" Judas said this, not because he cared for the poor, but because he was a thief; he was in charge of the money bag and took what was put in it.

"Leave her alone," Jesus responded. "She has kept this oil for the day of My burial. The poor you have with you always, but you do not have Me always."[30]

HIS TRIUMPHAL ENTRY INTO JERUSALEM

On the next day, when they drew near to Jerusalem and came to Bethphage, at the Mount of Olives, Jesus sent two of His disciples and said to them, "Go into the village over there. There you shall find a donkey tied and with her a colt that has never been ridden. Untie them and bring them to Me. If anyone asks you, 'Why do you untie them?' answer, 'Because the Lord needs them,' and he will send them here."

The disciples went their way and did as Jesus commanded them. They found the donkey and colt tied outside on the street, by the door, just as He had said to them, and they untied them.

Then some of them who stood there asked them, "What are you doing, untying the colt?" The disciples responded to them as Jesus had commanded, and they let the disciples go.

So the disciples brought the donkey and the colt to Jesus, put their coats on them, and set Him upon the colt.[31]

All this was done to fulfill what God had spoken through the prophet [Zechariah about 500 years earlier], saying, "Tell the daughter of Zion, 'Fear not. Look, your King comes to you, humble, and sitting on a donkey's colt.'"[32]

A very large crowd that was coming to the Passover feast heard that Jesus was coming to Jerusalem and went out to meet Him. Many spread their coats on the road, and some cut down branches of palm trees and spread them on the road.

Those who went ahead and those who followed shouted, "Hosanna [save us], O Son of David! Blessed is the King of Israel Who comes in the name of the Lord! Blessed be the kingdom of our father David! Hosanna [save us], O God Most High!"[33]

> *The meaning of the Hebrew word "hosanna" is "save us, we pray." The people surely meant, "Save us from the military occupation of the Roman Empire."*

When Jesus approached the foot of the Mount of Olives, the whole crowd of disciples began to rejoice and praise God with a loud voice for all the mighty works that they had seen, saying, "Blessed be the King that comes in the name of the Lord! Peace in heaven, and glory in the highest!"

Some of the Pharisees who were in the crowd said to Jesus, "Master, rebuke Your disciples."

He responded, "I tell you that if they would be quiet, the stones would immediately shout out loud."

When Jesus approached Jerusalem, He looked out over the city and openly wept over it.[34]

When He came into Jerusalem, the entire city was stirred with excitement, asking, "Who is this?"

The crowd answered, "This is Jesus, the prophet from Nazareth in Galilee."[35]

The Pharisees therefore said among themselves, "Do you see that we are accomplishing nothing? Look, the world has gone after Him!"[36]

Jesus went into the temple of God and looked around at what was happening. Then as evening drew near, He went out to Bethany with His twelve disciples.[37]

He Cleanses the Temple

The next day they came back to Jerusalem. Jesus went into the temple and began to drive out those who sold and bought in the temple. He overturned the tables of the moneychangers and the chairs of those who sold doves, and He would not allow anyone to carry something through the temple as a shortcut.

He taught, "It is written, 'All nations shall call My house the house of prayer';[38] but you have made it a den of thieves." The scribes and chief priests heard what He said.[39]

The blind and the lame came to Him in the temple, and He healed them. When the chief priests and scribes saw all the wonderful things He did, and the children shouting in the temple and saying, "Hosanna [save us], O Son of David!" they were very displeased. They wondered how they might get rid of Him, for they feared Him because the people were astonished at His teaching.[40]

In the evening, He left them and went out of the city to Bethany, and He stayed there.[41]

In the morning, He returned to the city and taught in the temple. The chief priests, the scribes, and the leaders of the people sought to get rid of Him. But they could not figure out what to do, for the people wanted to hear Him.[42]

THE CHIEF PRIESTS CONFRONT HIM

As Jesus taught the people in the temple and preached the good news, the chief priests, scribes, and elders confronted Him and demanded, "Tell us, by what authority do You do all these things, and who gave You this authority?" But Jesus did not answer them.[43]

That very hour they sought to arrest Him, for they understood that He had spoken against them in His teachings. However, they feared the people.[44]

So they watched Him, and sent out spies who pretended to be righteous men to try to catch Him in His words, so that they might deliver Him over to the power and authority of the Roman governor. Then they left Him and went on their way.[45]

Jesus said, "Now is the judgment of this world; now shall the prince of this world [Satan] be cast out. And I, if I be lifted up from the earth, will draw all people to Me." He said this to indicate how He would die [crucifixion].[46]

JESUS DELIBERATELY PREPARES FOR HIS DEATH 13

THE CHIEF PRIESTS PLOT TO KILL HIM

Now the Feast of Unleavened Bread, which is also called the Feast of Passover, approached. Jesus said to His disciples, "You know that the Feast of Unleavened Bread is in two days, and the Son of Man will be betrayed to be crucified."[47]

Then the chief priests, the scribes, and the elders of the people gathered together at the palace of the high priest, Caiaphas. They consulted as to how they might take Jesus by craftiness and subtlety and kill Him. But they said, "Let us not do it on the Feast Day [Passover high Sabbath], lest there be an uproar among the people," for they were afraid of the people.[48]

JESUS IS AGAIN ANOINTED FOR BURIAL

Jesus was in Bethany at the house of Simon the leper. As He sat at the table, a woman came having an alabaster [semi-precious stone] flask of very costly perfumed oil. She broke the flask and poured the oil on His head.

When His disciples saw it, they were indignant, saying to themselves, "Why this waste? For this fragrant oil might have been sold for more than three hundred denarii [Roman coins, about one year's wages] and given to the poor." So they criticized her sharply.

But Jesus told them to leave her alone. "Why do you trouble her?" He asked. "She has done Me a good service. For the poor are with you always, and whenever you wish you may do them good; but you do not have Me always. She has done what she could; she came ahead of time to anoint My body for burial. I tell you truly, wherever this gospel is preached throughout the whole world, what this woman has done will also be spoken of as a memorial to her."[49]

JUDAS ARRANGES TO BETRAY HIM

Then Satan entered into Judas (surnamed Iscariot), who was one of the twelve. So he went to the chief priests and discussed with them and the captains [Jewish temple guards] how he might betray Jesus to them.

He asked them, "What will you give me if I will deliver Him to you?" When they heard it, they were glad and promised to give him thirty pieces of silver [as had been prophesied by God through the prophet Zechariah about 500 years earlier].[50] So Judas promised them. From that day on, he sought a convenient time to betray Jesus to them in the absence of the crowd.[51]

JESUS TEACHES OPENLY IN THE TEMPLE

In the daytime Jesus was teaching in the temple, and at night He went out and stayed on the Mount of Olives, where there was a garden called Gethsemane [which means "olive-oil press"].

Early in the morning, all the people came to Him in the temple, to hear Him.[52] Jesus shouted, "He who believes in Me believes not just in Me, but also in Him Who sent Me; and he who sees Me sees Him Who sent Me. I have come as a light into the world, so that anyone who believes in Me should not live in darkness.

"If any man hears My words and does not believe them, I do not judge him; for I did not come to judge the world, but to save the world. He who rejects Me and does not receive My words is judged by what I have said, which shall judge him on the day of judgment. For I have not spoken My own words. Rather, the Father Who sent Me told Me what I should say. I know that His commandment is life everlasting. So I speak whatever the Father has said to Me."[53]

Explanations of the Feast of Passover and the Different Sabbaths

This section provides explanations that are very important in understanding the Jewish feast of Passover, the difference between the days that the Pharisees and the Sadducees kept the feast, the difference between the high Sabbaths and the weekly Sabbath, and on which day of the week Jesus was crucified.

- A Jewish day begins at sunset (not midnight) and ends at the following sunset.
- On the seventh day of each week, the Jews celebrated the Sabbath according to the fourth of the ten commandments God gave them.[54] "Sabbath" means "to cease, to rest." The Sabbath was a day of rest, which commemorated the fact that God rested on the seventh day after completing His creation.[55]
- The feast (or festival) of Passover, also called the Feast of Unleavened Bread, was one of the most important religious feasts in the Jewish year and was in their month of Nisan. The feast was for seven days.[56]
- Both the first day and the seventh day of the Feast of Passover were high Sabbaths or holy convocations (sacred assemblies).[57]

- The Preparation Day was the day before this feast, when they cleansed all leaven (yeast) out of their houses and killed and roasted the Passover lamb to eat at the Passover meal after sunset, which would be the beginning of the first high Sabbath.
- The blood of the Passover lamb was applied to the posts and the crosspiece of the door of each house at this sunset.[58]
- The Passover day was the first day of the feast and was the first high Sabbath. It was at the start of this day, after sunset, that they ate the Passover lamb with unleavened bread and other special items of the Passover meal. All that remained of the lamb had to be totally burnt before morning.
- The Jewish calendar was a lunar calendar; thus the special high Sabbaths could fall on any day of the week, depending on the year, whereas the regular weekly Sabbaths were always on the seventh day of each week.
- Two different Jewish calendars were in use in Jesus' time.
- The Pharisees and the Sadducees were the two main groups in Jewish religion and politics at Jesus' time, and their beliefs and customs were very different from each other.
- Most Pharisees observed the preparation day on the thirteenth day of Nisan and their Passover day (their first high Sabbath), on the fourteenth of Nisan.
- But most Sadducees observed their preparation day one day later, on the fourteenth of Nisan, and their Passover day (their first high Sabbath), on the fifteenth of Nisan.

- This enabled Jesus to eat the Passover meal with His disciples early on Nisan fourteenth, the Pharisees' Passover day, and then later on that same day to fulfill its prophetic symbolism (Himself, being God's Passover Lamb, sacrificed for us)[59] on the Sadducees' preparation day, when their Passover lamb was slain.
- The day after Jesus' crucifixion was the Sadducees' Passover high Sabbath. It was not the regular weekly Sabbath, as some people believe.
- Three full days and nights in the tomb before His resurrection on the first day of the week means that Jesus must have been crucified on the fourth day of the week and buried just before sunset, which was the beginning of the Sadducees' Passover high Sabbath.
- But on which day of the week Jesus was crucified is of little importance. The greatest significance, by far, is that Jesus, by His crucifixion, burial, and resurrection, atoned (paid the penalty) for the sins of the whole human race. And through this, God now offers to us all free, full forgiveness, loving acceptance, and eternal life.

THE CRUCIFIXION WEEK

Day of Week	3rd, begins at sunset	4th, begins at sunset	5th, begins at sunset	6th, begins at sunset	7th, begins at sunset	1st, begins at sunset
Day of Jewish Month	13th of Nisan	14th of Nisan	15th of Nisan	16th of Nisan	17th of Nisan	18th of Nisan
Passover Feast Day	Pharisees' preparation day	Pharisees' Passover high Sabbath; Sadducees' preparation day	Sadducees' Passover high Sabbath		Regular weekly Sabbath	
Events	Jesus and disciples prepare for the Passover supper	Jesus' Passover meal; Gethsemane agony, betrayal, and arrest; Jewish court trial; Roman court trial; Jesus is crucified; Jesus is buried	The chief priests and Pharisees ask for the tomb to be guarded; Jewish soldiers seal and guard the tomb	Jewish soldiers guard the tomb; women buy and prepare spices and oils to anoint Jesus' body	Jewish soldiers guard the tomb; everyone keeps the weekly Sabbath	Jesus is resurrected; the guards flee; women come to the tomb; Jesus appears to three women, Peter, two disciples, and ten of His apostles

CHAPTER THREE

JESUS' LAST PASSOVER SUPPER

HE PREPARES FOR THE SUPPER WITH HIS DISCIPLES

On the first day of the Feast of Unleavened Bread [the Pharisees' preparation day], when the Passover lamb had to be killed, Jesus' disciples came to Him and asked, "Where do You want us to go and prepare, so that You may eat the Passover meal?"

So He sent Peter and John, saying, "Go and prepare the Passover meal for us, that we may eat it. When you enter the city, a man carrying a pitcher of water will meet you. Follow him into the house where he enters. Say to the owner of the house, 'The Master says to you, "My time has come. Where is the guest chamber where I shall eat the Passover meal with My disciples?"' He will show you a large upper room furnished and prepared; make preparations for us there."

Those disciples went into the city and found everything just as He had said to them. And they prepared for the Passover meal.[60]

Now before the feast of the Passover, Jesus knew that the time had come when He would depart out of this world to the Father. Having loved those who were His own in the world, He loved them to the end.[61]

HIS PASSOVER SUPPER

So, at sunset [when the Pharisees' Passover high Sabbath began], He came with the twelve. When the time came, He sat down with the twelve apostles. He said to them, "I have greatly desired to eat this Passover meal with you before I suffer; for I tell you, I will not eat of it again until it is fulfilled in the kingdom of God."[62]

> *The Feast of Passover was a remembrance and celebration of how God delivered the Jews from bondage and slavery in Egypt many centuries before. The Passover lamb was killed, roasted in fire, and eaten at a very special supper after sundown. The blood of the lamb was applied to the doorway of their house, so that the judgment of God would "pass over" their household and save them from death.*
>
> *God had made this a prophetic picture of Jesus being His Passover Lamb. As Jesus ate the Passover meal with his apostles, He told them that this prophetic picture was about to be fulfilled. Jesus was then slain, and His blood was shed to atone (pay the penalty) for all our sin. Christ Himself is our Passover lamb, sacrificed for us.[63]*
>
> *Jesus' shed blood must now be spiritually applied to the "doorway" of our "hearts" by each one of us personally, by faith, receiving Him and His Astounding Sacrifice for our salvation.*

HE PREDICTS HIS BETRAYAL

As they sat and ate, Jesus said, "I tell you truly, one of you who eats with Me shall betray Me. Look, my betrayer is seated with Me at this table."[64]

So they began to ask among themselves which of them it was that would do this. They were very sad, and one by one they began to ask Him, "Is it I?"

He answered them, "It is one of the twelve, who dips his hand in the bowl with Me; he shall betray Me. The Son of Man goes as it is written of Him; but woe to the man by whom the Son of Man is betrayed! It would have been good for that man if he had not been born."[65]

Then Judas, who did betray Him, whispered to Him, "Master, is it I?"

"You said it yourself," Jesus answered.[66]

Jesus Establishes the New Covenant

At the end of the supper, Jesus took a pitcher of wine, gave thanks and said, "Take this, and divide it among you. I tell you truly, I will not drink the fruit of the vine again until the day that I drink it new in the kingdom of God."

He also took the unleavened bread and gave thanks, and blessed it, broke it, and gave it to them, saying, "Take and eat this. This is My body which is given and broken for you; do this in remembrance of Me."

In the same way He took the cup of wine, saying, "This cup is the new covenant in My blood, which is shed for you and for many, for the forgiveness of sins. As often as you drink it, do this in commemoration and celebration of Me. All of you drink it." And they all drank.[67]

He Demonstrates Astounding Humility

Now there was a rivalry among them as to which of them should be considered the greatest. So Jesus said to them, "The kings of the Gentiles lord it over them; and those who exercise authority over them are called 'benefactors.' But you must not be like that; rather, the one who is greatest among you, let him be as the youngest, and the one who is in charge, as he that serves. For who is greater, the one who sits at a meal or the one who serves? Is it not the one who sits at the meal? But I am among you as He Who serves.

"You are the ones who have continued with Me in My trials and temptations. I give you a kingdom, as My Father has given Me, so that you may eat and drink at My table in My kingdom and sit on thrones judging the twelve tribes of Israel."[68]

When supper was finished, the devil put into the heart of Judas Iscariot, Simon's son, to betray Him then.

Jesus, knowing that the Father had given Him everything and that He had come from God and went to God, arose from supper. He laid aside His robe and took a towel and wrapped Himself. Then He poured water into a basin and began to wash the disciples' feet and to wipe them with the towel wrapped around Him.

When He came to Simon Peter, Peter objected, saying to Him, "Lord, do You plan to wash my feet?"

"Now you do not understand what I am doing, but you shall understand it afterwards," answered Jesus.

"You shall never wash my feet," protested Peter.

Jesus responded, "If I do not wash your feet, you have no part with Me."

So Simon Peter said to Him, "Lord, then do not wash my

feet only, but also my hands and my head."

"He that has bathed needs only to wash his feet in order to be fully clean," replied Jesus. "But not all of you are clean."

Jesus said "not all of you are clean" because He knew who would betray Him.[69]

JESUS TEACHES HIS DISCIPLES HIS HUMILITY

So after He had washed their feet and had put on His robe and sat down again, He said to them, "Do you know what I have done to you? You call Me Master and Lord; you say well, for so I am. So if I, your Lord and Master, have washed your feet, you also ought to wash one another's feet. I have given you an example that you should do as I have done to you. I tell you truly, the servant is not greater than his lord; nor is the one who is sent greater than the one who sent him. If you know these things, you will be happy if you do them."[70]

HE AGAIN PREDICTS HIS BETRAYAL

"I am not talking about all of you; I know whom I have chosen. But the Scripture [as God had prophesied to the prophet David, about 1,000 years earlier] must be fulfilled: 'He who dines with Me has turned against Me.'[71] Now I tell you before it happens, so that when it happens you may believe that I am He. I tell you truly, whoever receives the one I send receives Me; and whoever receives Me receives Him Who sent Me." When Jesus said this, He was troubled in spirit and declared, "Believe Me, one of you shall betray Me."

Then the disciples looked at one another, wondering of whom He spoke. Now leaning on Jesus' chest was one of His disciples, John, whom Jesus loved. So, Simon Peter motioned to him that he should ask Jesus who it was.

He then reclined on Jesus' chest and whispered to Him, "Lord, who is it?"

Jesus whispered, "The one to whom I shall give a piece of bread when I have dipped it in the bowl." And when He had dipped the bread, He gave it to Judas Iscariot, the son of Simon. After that, Satan entered into Judas.

Then Jesus said to Judas, "What you are about to do, do it quickly." Now no one at the table knew why He said this to Judas. Some of them thought that since Judas was in charge of the moneybag, Jesus had told him to buy things they would need for the feast or that he should give something to the poor. As soon as he ate the piece of bread, Judas left.

It was night.[72]

Jesus Gives His Great New Commandment

When Judas left, Jesus said, "Now comes the glory of the Son of Man, and in His glory God is exalted. Since God is exalted in His glory, God will glorify Him without delay. My dear ones, I am with you yet for a short time. You shall seek Me, but as I said to the Jews, 'Where I go, you cannot come'; so now I say the same thing to you.

"A new commandment I give you, that you love one another; as I have loved you, you should also love one another. By this shall everyone know that you are My disciples, if you love one another."[73]

He Predicts Peter's Denial

Simon Peter asked Him, "Lord, where are You going?"

Jesus answered, "Now you cannot follow Me where I go, but you shall follow Me afterwards."

"Lord, why can't I follow You now?" Peter asked. "I will lay down my life for Your sake."

"Will you lay down your life for My sake?" Jesus asked. "Believe Me, the rooster shall not crow twice until you have denied Me three times."[74]

Jesus Declares That He Is the Only Way to the Father

"Don't be troubled; if you believe in God, believe in Me, too. In My Father's house are many dwelling places; I would have told you if that were not so. If I go and prepare a place for you, I will come again and receive you to Myself; that you may be where I am. And you know both where I am going and the way there."

Thomas said to Him, "Lord, we do not know where You are going, so how can we know the way?"

Jesus responded, "I am the way [to the Father], the truth [about the Father], and the life [of the Father]. No man comes to the Father except through Me. If you had known Me, you also would have known My Father; and from now on, you know Him and have seen Him."

Philip said to Him, "Lord, show us the Father, and we will be satisfied."

"Have I been with you all this time, and yet you have not known Me, Philip?" Jesus answered. "He who has seen Me has seen the Father. So how can you say, 'Show us the Father'? Do you not believe that I am in the Father, and the Father in Me? My words to you are not spoken on My own authority, but the Father Who dwells in Me does the work. Believe Me that I am in the Father and the Father in Me, or else believe Me for the sake of the works I am doing.

I tell you truly, he who believes in Me will also do the works that I do, and even greater works than these, because I go to My Father. And whatever you shall ask in My name, I will do it, so that the Father may be glorified in the Son. If you ask anything in My name, I will do it."[75]

HE PROMISES TO SEND THE HOLY SPIRIT

"If you love Me, keep My commandments. And I will ask the Father, and He shall give you another Comforter [Strength-giver] to live with you forever. This is the Spirit of Truth Whom the world cannot receive, because it does not see or know Him. But you know Him, for He lives with you and shall be in you. I will not leave you comfortless [fatherless]; I will come to you.

"After a short time, the world will see Me no more; but you see Me. Because I live, you shall live also. Then you shall know that I am in My Father, and that you are in Me and I am in you. Whoever has My commandments and keeps them is the one who loves Me; and whoever loves Me shall be loved by My Father, and I will love him and show Myself to him."[76]

Judas (not Iscariot) asked Him, "Lord, how will You show Yourself to us, and not to the world?"

Jesus answered, "If someone loves Me, he will follow My teaching, and My Father will love him, and We will come to him and live with him. Anyone who does not love Me does not follow My teaching; and what you hear Me speak is not My words, but the words of the Father Who sent Me. These things I have spoken to you while I am with you. But the Comforter [Strength-giver], Who is the Holy Spirit, Whom the Father will send in My name, He shall teach you all things and remind you of what I have said to you.

"Peace I leave with you, My peace I give to you; the peace I give you is not what the world gives. Don't be troubled or afraid. You have heard Me tell you, 'I go away, and come again to you.' If you loved Me, you would rejoice because I said, 'I go to the Father,' for My Father is greater than I. Now I have told you beforehand, so that when it happens, you might believe. From now on I will not talk much with you, for the prince of this world [Satan] comes; but he has no claim on Me. I am doing what the Father commanded Me, so that the world may know that I love the Father."[77]

HE AGAIN PREDICTS PETER'S DENIAL

The Lord said, "Simon Peter, Satan has wanted to possess you, that he may sift you as wheat; but I have prayed for you, that your faith will not fail. When you turn back to Me, strengthen your brothers."

But Peter protested, "Lord, I am ready to go with You, both into prison and to death."

"I tell you, Peter," Jesus responded, "the rooster shall not crow twice today before you will deny three times that you know Me."[78]

He said to them all, "When I sent you without a money bag, packsack, and extra sandals, did you lack any thing?"

"Nothing," they answered.

Then He said to them, "But now, he who has a money bag, let him take it, and also his packsack. And he who has no sword, let him sell his coat and buy one. For I tell you that what is written [by the prophet Isaiah, about 700 years earlier] must yet be accomplished in Me: 'And He was numbered among the transgressors.'[79] For there is a purpose underlying the things concerning Me."

They said, "Lord, here are two swords."

"That is enough," He answered.[80]

JESUS DECLARES THAT HE IS THE TRUE VINE

When they had sung a hymn, Jesus left and, as He was accustomed, went to go to the Mount of Olives, followed by His disciples.[81]

As they went [through the city], Jesus said to them, "I am the true vine, and My Father is the vinedresser. He takes away every branch in Me that does not bear fruit, and He prunes every branch that bears fruit, so that it may produce more fruit. Now you are pruned [clean] through the word that I have spoken to you.

"Remain in Me, and I will remain in you. As the branch cannot bear fruit by itself unless it is attached to the vine, neither can you bear fruit unless you remain in Me. I am the vine; you are the branches. Whoever remains in Me, and I in him, produces much fruit; for without Me you can do nothing. Anyone who does not remain in Me is cast out as a [dead] branch and withers; and dead branches are gathered and cast into the fire where they are burned. If you remain in Me and My words remain in you, whatever you ask for shall be done for you. My Father is glorified when you bear much fruit; in this way shall you be My disciples.

"Just as the Father has loved Me, I have loved you; remain in My love. If you keep My commandments, you shall remain in My love, just as I have kept My Father's commandments and remain in His love. I told you this so that My joy might remain in you, and your joy might be full. My commandment is that you love one another, as I have loved you.

"Greater love has no man than this, that a man would sacrifice his life for his friends. You are My friends if you keep My commands. From now on, I do not call you servants; for the servant does not know what his master is doing. But I have called you My friends, for I have told you everything that I have heard from My Father. You have not chosen Me, but I have chosen you and appointed you to go and bear fruit—fruit that remains—that whatever you ask the Father in My name, He may give it to you.

"I command you to love one another."[82]

HE PREDICTS PERSECUTION

"If the world hates you, know that it hated Me first. The world would love you if you were of the world. But the world hates you because you are not of the world, because I have chosen you out of the world. Remember what I told you, 'The servant is not greater than his master.' If they have persecuted Me, they will also persecute you; if they have kept My sayings, they will keep yours also. But what they do to you will be for My name's sake, because they do not know Him that sent Me.

"If I had not come and spoken to them, they would not have had so much sin; but now they have no covering for their sin. Anyone who hates Me, hates My Father also. If I had not done among them works which no one else did, they would not have had so much sin; but now they have both seen and hated both Me and My Father. But this happens to fulfill what is written in their law [by the prophet David, about 1,000 years earlier]: 'They hated Me without a cause.'"[83]

JESUS AGAIN PROMISES TO SEND THE HOLY SPIRIT

"But when the Comforter [Strength-giver] comes, He shall proclaim the truth about Me; He is the Spirit of Truth Who proceeds from the Father, Whom I will send to you from the Father. And you also shall bear witness, because you have been with Me from the beginning.[84]

"I have told you these things so that you should not be offended. They shall throw you out of the synagogues [Jewish religious meeting places]. Yes, the time will come when whoever kills you will think that he does God a service. They will do this to you because they have not known the Father, or Me. I have told you these things so that when the time comes, you may remember that I told you of them.

"I did not tell you this at the beginning, because I was with you; but now I am going to Him Who sent Me. None of you asks Me, 'Where are You going?' But because I have said these things to you, sorrow has filled your heart. However, believe Me that it is better for you that I go away, for if I do not go away, the Comforter [Strength-giver] will not come to you. But if I leave, I will send Him to you. When He comes, He will convict the world of sin and righteousness, and warn of judgment: of sin, because they do not believe in Me; of righteousness, because I go to the Father and you see Me no more; of judgment, because the prince of this world [Satan] is judged.

"I still have many things to tell you, but you cannot comprehend them now. But when the Spirit of Truth comes, He will guide you into all truth. He shall not speak of Himself, but He will speak whatever He hears and will show you things to come.

"He shall glorify Me, for He will take what is Mine and show it to you. Everything that My Father has is Mine. That is why I said that He shall take what is Mine and show it to you."[85]

JESUS PREDICTS THAT HE WILL RETURN TO THE FATHER

"In a short time, you shall not see Me; and after another short time you shall see Me, because I go to the Father."

Then some of His disciples said among themselves, "What does He mean, 'In a short time, you shall not see Me; and after another short time you shall see Me' and, 'Because I go to the Father'? What does He mean, 'In a short time'? We do not understand what He is saying."

Now, Jesus knew that they wanted to ask Him about this. So He said to them, "Are you asking among yourselves why I said, 'In a short time, you shall not see Me; and after another short time and you shall see Me'? Believe Me, you shall weep and mourn, but the world shall rejoice; and you shall be sorrowful, but your sorrow shall be turned into joy. A woman in the pain of childbirth is in anguish when the time to deliver her baby arrives. But as soon as she has delivered the child, she no longer remembers the anguish because of the joy that a baby has been born into the world. So now you are sorrowful. But I will see you again, and your heart shall rejoice; and no one will take your joy away from you.

"Believe Me, the Father will give you whatever you shall ask Him in My name. Until now, you have asked nothing in My name. Ask Him, and you shall receive, that your joy may be full.

"I spoke these things to you in metaphors. But the time will come when I shall no longer speak to you in figurative language, but I shall show you the Father plainly. Then, you shall ask the

Father in My name. I am not saying that I will pray to the Father for you; for the Father Himself loves you because you have loved Me and have believed that I came from God. I came from the Father and have come into the world. Now I leave the world and go to the Father."

His disciples said to Him, "Look, now You speak plainly rather than in metaphors. Now we are sure that You know all things and do not need anyone to instruct You. By this we believe that You came from God."

"Now you believe?" Jesus responded. "Look, the hour comes and has even arrived when you shall be scattered, every man to his own, and shall leave Me alone. However, I am not alone, because the Father is with Me. I have told you these things so that in Me you might have peace. In the world you shall have tribulation, but be comforted; I have overcome the world."[86]

HE PREDICTS PETER'S DENIAL FOR THE THIRD TIME

Then Jesus said to them, "All of you shall desert Me tonight; for it is written [by the prophet Zechariah, about 500 years earlier], 'I will strike the shepherd, and the sheep of the flock shall be scattered abroad.'[87] But I will go before you into Galilee after I have risen again."

Peter protested, "I will never desert You even if everyone else is offended because of You."

"Believe Me," Jesus responded, "this very night, before the rooster crows twice, you shall deny Me three times."

But Peter insisted vehemently, "If I should die with You, I will not deny You in any way." All the disciples said likewise.[88]

Jesus' Great Prayer for His Disciples, and for Us All

Then Jesus lifted up His eyes to heaven and said, "Father, the time has come. Glorify Your Son, that Your Son may also glorify You. You have given Him power over all people, that He should give eternal life to as many as You have given Him. This is eternal life, that they might know You, the only true God, and Jesus Christ, the Messiah, Whom You have sent. I have glorified You on the earth. I have finished the work which You gave Me to do. Now, O Father, glorify Me with the glory which I had with You before the world was created.

"I have shown Your character and nature to those whom You gave Me out of the world. They were Yours, and you gave them to Me, and they have obeyed Your commands. Now they know that everything You have given Me is of You, for I have given them the words you gave Me. They have received My words, known with certainty that I came from You, and believed that You sent Me.

"I pray for them. I do not pray for everyone, but for those whom You have given to Me, for they are Yours. All that are Mine are Yours, and Yours are Mine, and I am glorified in them. Now I am leaving here and I come to You, but these ones are still here. Holy Father, keep those whom You have given Me through Your Own name, that they may be one, as We are one. While I was here with them, I kept them in Your name. Those whom You gave Me I have kept, and none of them is lost except the son of destruction [Judas], that the Scripture might be fulfilled.[89]

"Now I come to You. These things I speak while I am here, so that My joy might be fulfilled in them; I have given them Your word. The world has hated them because they are not of the world, just as I am not of the world. I do not pray that You take them out of the world, but that You keep them from the evil one [Satan]. They are not of the world, just as I am not of the world.

"Perfect them through Your truth. Your word is truth. Just as You have sent Me into the world, I have also sent them into the world. For their sakes I keep Myself holy, so that they also might be made holy through the truth.

"I pray not just for these, but also for those who shall believe in Me through their word: that they all may be one, as You, Father, are in Me, and I in You; that they also may be one in Us, that the world may believe that You have sent Me. I have given them the glory You gave Me, so that they may be one, even as We are one: I in them, and You in Me, that they may be made perfect in unity, and that the world may know that You have sent Me and have loved them as you have loved Me.

"Father, I want to have those whom You have given Me with Me, that they may see the glory that You have given Me, for You loved Me before the foundation of the world. O righteous Father, the world has not known You, but I have known You; and these have known that You have sent Me. I have revealed to them Your character and nature, and will reveal it, that Your love for Me may be in them, and I in them."[90]

Chapter Four

Jesus' Astounding Submission

His Great Agony in Gethsemane

W hen He had said this, Jesus went with His disciples over the brook Kidron. There they entered a garden called Gethsemane [which means "olive-oil press"]. Judas, who betrayed Him, also knew the place; for Jesus often went there with His disciples.[91]

When He arrived, Jesus said to His disciples, "Sit here, while I go and pray over there. Pray that you do not fail in the testing." He took with Him Peter as well as James and John, the two sons of Zebedee.

Then He became troubled and deeply distressed, and said to them, "My soul is extremely troubled, even to the point of death. Wait here, and be on the alert with Me."[92]

Jesus Pleads Three Times with the Father

He went a little farther forward from them, about a stone's throw away, kneeled down, prostrated Himself with His face on the ground and prayed that, if it were possible, the ordeal might pass from Him. He prayed, "O Abba [Papa], My Father, if it be possible, let this cup pass from Me [relieve Me of this task]; nevertheless, not as I will, but as You will."

Jesus knew well ahead of this moment what the Father was asking Him to do. Being fully human (as well as divine) Jesus' sinless soul naturally was recoiling from the horrible ordeal that He was about to go through—all the humiliating shame and abuse, all the torturous suffering and pain—and especially recoiling from bearing all the guilt and condemnation of the vileness, evil, and sin of mankind.

Hebrews 5:7 says that Christ prayed, crying aloud and weeping as He pleaded with Him Who was able to save Him from death. According to the Gospels, Jesus prayed this way three times.

The Father's astounding answer to Jesus' agony and pleading must have been, each time, "No, My dear Son, there is no other possible way for Us to redeem mankind, forgive all their sin, reconcile them back to Us, and give them eternal life."

Although Jesus prayed to be saved from death, each time Jesus prayed, He said to the Father, "Nevertheless, not My will, but Yours be done." Thus Philippians 2:8 says that as a man, Jesus humbled Himself and became obedient to the point of death, even the death of the cross.

He came back to the disciples and found them sound asleep. He said to Peter, "Simon, are you sleeping? Could you not watch and stay awake with Me for one hour? Why are you sleeping? Get up, watch and pray, so that you do not fail in the testing. The spirit truly is ready and willing, but the flesh is weak."

He went away again the second time and prayed the same words, saying, "Abba, [Papa] Father, all things are possible for You. Take away this cup from Me [relieve Me of this task]; nevertheless, not what I will, but what You will."

An angel from heaven appeared, strengthening Him. Being in agony, He prayed more earnestly, and His sweat was like great drops of blood falling down to the ground.

Then He returned to the disciples and found them asleep again, for they could not keep their eyes open. They did not know what to say to Him. So He left them, went away again, and prayed the third time, saying the same words, "O My Father, if this cup may not pass away from Me, but I must drink it [if I may not be relieved of this task, but I must complete it], Your will be done."[93]

Jesus Accepts the Father's Final Answer

When He rose up from prayer and had come back to His disciples the third time, He said to them, "Are you still sleeping and resting? It is enough! Look, the time has come, and the Son of Man is being betrayed into the hands of sinners. Get up, let us go. Look, my betrayer is very near."[94]

CHAPTER FIVE

JESUS IS BETRAYED

JUDAS BETRAYS HIM WITH A KISS

While He spoke, Judas, one of the twelve, came with a band of men and officers from the chief priests, scribes, Pharisees, and elders. This crowd came with lanterns, torches, swords, and clubs.

Jesus, knowing what would happen to Him, went forward and asked them, "Whom do you seek?"

Now his betrayer had given them a sign, saying, "Whoever I shall kiss, that is the One. Take Him, hold Him tight, and lead Him away safely."

So Judas went ahead of them and drew near to Jesus to kiss Him. He said, "Greetings, Master," and then kissed Him.

"Friend, why have you come?" Jesus asked. "Do you betray the Son of Man with a kiss?"[95]

Then Judas, who betrayed Him, went and stood with the band of officers.

Jesus asked them, "Whom do you seek?"

"Jesus of Nazareth," they answered.

Jesus responded, "I am He." As soon as He had said this to them, they staggered backwards and fell to the ground. Then He asked them again, "Whom do you seek?"

"Jesus of Nazareth," they answered.

"I have told you that I am He," Jesus responded. "If it is Me you seek, let My disciples go their way." He said this to fulfill what He had spoken:[96] "I have lost none of those You gave Me."[97]

Then they came to arrest Jesus and take Him.[98]

Peter Tries to Defend Jesus

When those who were around Jesus saw what was happening, they asked Him, "Lord, shall we strike with the sword?" Having a sword, Simon Peter suddenly drew it and struck the high priest's servant, cutting off his right ear. The servant's name was Malchus.

Then Jesus said to Peter, "Allow this much to happen. Put your sword back into its sheath, for all those who draw the sword shall die by the sword. Don't you think that I can now pray to My Father, and He would immediately give Me more than twelve legions of angels [36,000 to 72,000 angels]?[99] But in that case, how shall the Scriptures be fulfilled, that it must happen this way?[100] Shall I not drink the cup My Father has given Me?"[101]

And Jesus touched Malchus' ear and healed him.

At the same time, Jesus said to the crowd who had come to Him, "Have you come out as against a thief, with swords and clubs, to arrest Me? I sat daily with you teaching in the temple, and you did not arrest Me. But this is the time for you and the power of darkness, and it is occurring to fulfill the Scriptures, as foretold by the prophets."[102]

JESUS GIVES HIMSELF OVER TO THE MOB

Then all the disciples deserted Him and fled.[103] One of His followers was a certain young man who had a linen cloak wrapped around his body. The young men grabbed him, and he left the linen cloak and fled from them.[104]

Then the crowd and the captain and officers of the Jews took Jesus, bound Him, and led Him away first to Annas, for he was father-in-law to Caiaphas, who was the high priest that year.[105]

PETER DENIES JESUS

Simon Peter followed Jesus afar off, as did another disciple, John, who was known by the high priest. John went in with Jesus into the palace of the high priest, but Peter stood at the door outside. Then John went out and spoke to the maid who kept the door, and brought in Peter.

The maid asked Peter, "Aren't you also one of Jesus' disciples?"

Peter answered, "I am not."

The servants and officers who stood there had made a fire of coals in the middle of the outer court below the palace, for it was cold. They sat down together and warmed themselves, and Peter stood with them and warmed himself.[106]

JESUS IS INTERROGATED BY ANNAS

The [former] high priest, Annas, then asked Jesus about His disciples and about His teaching.

Jesus answered him, "I spoke openly to everyone; I always taught in the synagogues and in the temple where the Jews meet.

I did not say anything in secret. So, why do you ask Me? Ask those who heard Me what I told them. They know what I said."

When He said this, one of the officers who stood by slapped Jesus with the palm of his hand, saying, "Do You answer a high priest this way?"

"If I have said anything wrong, tell Me," Jesus responded. "But if not, why do you hit Me?"[107]

JESUS IS INTERROGATED BY CAIAPHAS, THE HIGH PRIEST

Then Annas sent Jesus, Who was still bound, to Caiaphas, the high priest.[108] Caiaphas was the one who had counseled the Jews that it was best that one man should die for the people.[109] They brought Jesus into the high priest's house, where all the chief priests, the scribes, and the elders were assembled.

Peter followed Him afar off, into the palace of the high priest. The servants had kindled a fire in the middle of the courtyard and had sat down together. Peter went in and sat down among the servants and warmed himself at the fire, to see the outcome.[110]

PETER DENIES JESUS AGAIN

Then one of the maids of the high priest came and saw Peter warming himself. She looked at him intently and said, "You also were with Jesus of Nazareth in Galilee."

He denied Jesus before them all, saying, "Woman, I do not know Him. I don't know nor understand what you mean."

He went out into the porch; and the rooster crowed.

Then another maid saw him and said to those who stood by, "This fellow was also with Jesus of Nazareth. He is one of them."

So they asked him, "Are you also one of His disciples?"

Again he denied with an oath, saying, "No, I am not. I do not know the Man."[111]

PETER DENIES HIM THE THIRD TIME

About one hour later, those that stood by came to Peter and said again to him, "Surely you also are one of His disciples, for you are a Galilean; your accent betrays you."

Another confidently affirmed, "I am sure this fellow was with Him, for he is a Galilean."

One of the servants of the high priest, being a relative of the man whose ear Peter had cut off, said, "Didn't I see you in the garden with Him?"

Peter began to curse and swear, and denied again, saying, "I don't know what you mean. I do not know this Man you are talking about."

While he was still speaking, the rooster crowed the second time. The Lord turned and looked at Peter. Then Peter remembered the words of the Lord, how He had said to him, "Before the rooster crows twice, you shall deny Me three times." So Peter left; and when he thought about this, he wept bitterly.[112]

Chapter Six

Jesus Is Tried and Condemned

Jesus Is Tried by the Jewish Court

Just before daybreak [on the Sadducees' Passover preparation day], the elders of the people, the chief priests, and the scribes came together and led Him into their council.[113]

Then the chief priests, elders, and all the council sought false witness against Jesus. Even though many false witnesses came, they were not useful, because their testimonies contradicted each other. Finally, two false witnesses came and testified, "This Fellow said, 'I am able to destroy the temple of God that is made with hands and build another made without hands in three days.'" But even their testimonies did not agree.

So the high priest stood up in the midst of them and asked Jesus, "Do You have no answer to what is being testified against You?" But He kept silent and did not answer.[114]

Jesus Declares That He Is the Messiah, the Son of God

Again the high priest asked Him, "I command You by the Living God that You tell us if You are the Christ, the Messiah, the Son of the blessed God."

> *"Christ" is the Greek word for the Hebrew word "Messiah." The Hebrew word "Messiah" means the promised one, who is commissioned and sent from God to save His people.*

Jesus said to them, "If I tell you, you will not believe; and if I ask you [questions], you will not answer Me nor let Me go. I am as you have said; and afterwards you will see the Son of Man sitting at the right hand of Almighty God and coming in the clouds of heaven."

"Then are You the Son of God?" they all asked.

"It is as you said," Jesus answered.[115]

JESUS IS DECLARED GUILTY OF BLASPHEMY

Then the high priest tore his clothes [a sign of great distress], saying, "He has blasphemed. Why do we need any witnesses? For we ourselves have heard Him say it Himself. Look, you have heard His blasphemy just now. What do you think?"

"He is guilty of death," they answered.[116]

So as the morning dawned, the chief priests held a consultation with the elders and scribes and the whole council. And all the chief priests and elders of the people decided that Jesus should be put to death.[117]

HE IS MOCKED AND ABUSED

The men who held Jesus mocked Him and punched Him. Some began to spit on Him, and the servants slapped Him with the palms of their hands. They blindfolded Him and then slapped Him on the face, beat Him, and asked Him, "Prophesy to us, You Christ, Messiah; who struck You?" And they said many other blasphemous things against Him.[118]

> *This fulfilled what God spoke through the prophet Isaiah about 700 years earlier: "I gave My back to those who struck Me, and My cheeks to those who plucked off My beard. I did not hide My face from shame and spitting."[119] Isaiah also prophesied, saying, "His appearance was marred more than that of any man."[120]*

JESUS IS THEN TRIED BY PILATE, THE ROMAN GOVERNOR

Then the whole crowd arose. When they had bound Jesus, they led Him away to the hall of judgment and delivered Him to Pontius Pilate, the Roman governor. It was early [in the morning]. They themselves did not go into the judgment hall, so that they would not become defiled and then be unable to eat the Passover meal [the next day, which would be the Sadducees' Passover high Sabbath].[121]

So Pilate went out to them and asked, "Of what do you accuse this Man?"

"If He were not an evildoer, we would not have delivered Him up to you," they answered.

Then Pilate said to them, "You take Him and judge Him according to your law."

"It is not lawful for us to put any man to death," the Jews responded. This happened to fulfill what Jesus had said regarding the way He would die [crucifixion].[122]

Then they began to accuse Him, saying, "We found this Fellow perverting the nation and forbidding paying taxes to Caesar [the Roman emperor], saying that He Himself is Christ, the Messiah, a King."

So Pilate went into the judgment hall again, and called Jesus and asked Him, "Are You the King of the Jews?"

Jesus answered, "Is this what you say, or did others tell it to you about Me?"

"Am I a Jew?" Pilate responded. "Your own nation and the chief priests have delivered You to me. What have You done?"

"My kingdom is not of this world," Jesus answered. "If My kingdom were of this world, then My servants would fight so that I should not be delivered to the Jews; but My kingdom is not from here."

"Then You are a King," Pilate said.

"As you say, I am a King," Jesus answered. "To this end I was born, and for this reason I came into the world, that I should bear witness to the truth. Everyone that is of the truth hears My voice."

"What is truth?" asked Pilate.[123]

PILATE DECLARES JESUS' INNOCENCE

When Pilate had said this, he took Jesus and went out again to the Jews and said to them, "I find no fault at all in Him."[124]

Then the chief priests and elders accused Him of many things, but Jesus did not respond. So Pilate asked Him again, "Do you have nothing to say? See how many things they testify against You." Jesus still said nothing, so that Pilate was amazed.[125]

> So God's prophecy through Isaiah about 700 years earlier came to pass: "He was treated violently and He was afflicted, yet He said nothing."[126]

Pilate Again Declares Jesus' Innocence

Then Pilate said to the chief priests and the people, "I find no fault in this Man."

But the chief priests and the people became fiercer, saying, "He stirs up the people, teaching throughout all Judea, from Galilee all the way to Jerusalem."[127]

Jesus Is Sent to King Herod and Is Mocked Again

When they mentioned Galilee, Pilate asked whether Jesus was a Galilean. As soon as he knew that Jesus was under Herod's jurisdiction, he sent Him to Herod, who was also at Jerusalem then.

Herod was very glad when he saw Jesus. He had wanted to see Him for a long time, because he had heard many things about Him and he hoped to see Him perform a miracle. Herod questioned Him for a long time, but Jesus did not respond.

The chief priests and scribes stood and accused Him vehemently. Herod and his soldiers treated Him with contempt, mocked Him, clothed Him in a gorgeous robe, and sent Him back to Pilate. That very day Pilate and Herod became friends, although before this there had been enmity between them.[128]

Jesus Again Is Declared Innocent by Pilate

Pilate called together the chief priests, the rulers, and the people, and then said to them, "You have brought this Man to me as One that misleads the people. Look, I examined Him before you but have found no fault in Him based on your accusations. No, neither has Herod, after I sent you to him. Look, nothing worthy of death has been done by Him. I will therefore punish Him and release Him."[129]

PILATE TRIES TO RELEASE JESUS

Now at that feast [Passover], the governor [Pilate] was accustomed to releasing to the people a prisoner of their choice.

So Pilate said, "You have a custom that I should release to you a prisoner at the Passover."

The crowd shouted loudly that he should do as he had always done.

Pilate answered them, "Do you want me to release to you the King of the Jews?" He said this because he knew that the chief priests had turned Him in because they were jealous of Him.

At that time there was an infamous prisoner called Barabbas, a robber, who was held in prison along with others who, with him, had caused an uprising in the city. Barabbas had committed murder in the uprising.

The chief priests and elders persuaded the crowd and incited the people that they should rather ask for Barabbas to be released and for Jesus to be killed. So they all shouted together, "Away with this Man, and release Barabbas to us!"

But Pilate, wanting to release Jesus, asked them, "Which of the two do you want me to release to you?"

"Barabbas! Not this Man, but Barabbas!" they all shouted again.

"Then what shall I do with Jesus, Who is called Christ, the Messiah, Whom you call the King of the Jews?" Pilate asked.

"Let Him be crucified! Crucify Him! Crucify Him!" they all shouted.

Then Pilate said to them the third time, "Why, what evil has He done? I have found no reason to put him to death. So, I will punish Him and let Him go."

But they cried out even more, "Let Him be crucified! Crucify Him!" And they were insistent with loud shouts, demanding that He be crucified.[130]

Jesus Is Whipped and Then Mocked Again

Then Pilate ordered that Jesus be whipped.[131]

> So the prophecy of God in the Psalms was fulfilled: "The plowers made long furrows in My back."[132]

Pilate's soldiers then took Jesus into their common hall, called the Praetorium, and gathered the whole band of soldiers around Him. They stripped Him, whipped Him, and put a purple robe on Him. They wove a crown of thorns and pressed it on His head and put a rod [as a king's scepter] in His right hand. Then they bowed their knees before Him, mocked Him, and began to address Him, saying, "Greetings, King of the Jews!"

They also struck Him with their hands, spat on Him, and took the rod and hit Him on the head. Bowing their knees, they pretended to worship Him.[133]

Pilate Declares Jesus' Innocence
for the Fourth Time

Then Pilate went out again and said to the people, "Look, I bring Him out to you, so that you may know that I find no fault in

Him." Then Jesus came out, wearing the crown of thorns and the purple robe. And Pilate said to them, "Look, here is the Man!"[134]

But the Priests and the People Protest

When the chief priests and officers saw Him, they shouted out, "Crucify Him, crucify Him!"

"You take Him and crucify Him, for I find no fault in Him," Pilate retorted.

The Jews answered, "We have a law, and by our law He ought to die, because He called Himself the Son of God."

When Pilate heard that, he was even more afraid. So he went into the judgment hall again and asked Jesus, "Where do You come from?"

But Jesus did not reply. Then Pilate said to Him, "Do You not answer me? Don't You know that I have power to crucify You and power to release You?"

"You could have no power at all over Me unless it had been given to you from above," Jesus answered. "For that reason, the one that delivered Me to you has the greater sin."[135]

Pilate Again Tries to Release Jesus

From then on, Pilate sought to release Him. But the Jews shouted, "If you let this Man go, You are not a friend of Caesar [the Roman emperor]. Whoever makes himself a king speaks against Caesar."[136]

The Priests and the People Finally Prevail

When Pilate heard that, he brought Jesus out and sat down in the judgment seat in a place that is called the Pavement; in Hebrew, it is called Gabbatha.

When he had sat down on the judgment seat, his wife sent to him, saying, "Have nothing to do with that righteous Man; for I have been extremely troubled today because of a dream I had about Him last night."

Now it was the preparation day of the Passover [according to the Sadducees' tradition], and about the sixth hour [Roman civil time, about the third hour Jewish time, or about 9:00 a.m.]. Pilate said to the Jews, "Look, here is your King!"

But they shouted out, "Away with Him, away with Him. Crucify Him!"

"What, shall I crucify your King?" Pilate asked.

"We have no king but Caesar," the chief priests answered.[137]

And the voices of the rulers of the people and the chief priests were stronger.[138]

Barabbas, the Murderer,
Is Released Instead of Jesus

When Pilate saw that he could not prevail, but that instead a riot was starting, he took water and washed his hands before the crowd, saying, "I am innocent of the blood of this righteous Person. You handle it."

Then all the people shouted, "His blood be on us, and our children."

So Pilate, wanting to satisfy the people, gave sentence that it should be as they demanded: He released Barabbas, who had been cast into prison charged with insurrection and murder, and he delivered Jesus to their will.[139]

Chapter Seven

Jesus' Astounding Sacrifice

Jesus Is Sentenced to Be Crucified

P ilate then delivered Jesus to them to be crucified. So the Roman soldiers took Jesus and, after they had mocked him, took the purple robe off Him, put His own clothes on Him, and led Him away to crucify Him.[140]

Jesus Begins to Carry His Cross to the "Place of a Skull"

Then Jesus, carrying His cross, went out towards the "Place of a Skull," which in Hebrew is called Golgotha or [in Greek] Calvary. As they came out of the city, they found a man from Cyrene, Simon by name (the father of Alexander and Rufus), who was passing by, coming out of the countryside. They grabbed him, laid the cross on him, and compelled him to carry Jesus' cross after Him.[141]

He Predicts a Time of Great Trouble

Following Jesus was a large crowd of people and, among them, women who wept and mourned for Him. Turning to them,

Jesus said, "Daughters of Jerusalem, do not cry for Me, but cry for yourselves and your children. For the days are coming when they shall say, 'Blessed are the barren women, and the wombs that never bore babies, and the breasts that never nursed infants.' Then they shall say to the mountains, 'Fall on us' and to the hills, 'Cover us.' For if they do these things in a green tree [during a favorable time], what shall be done in the dry [during a difficult time]?"[142]

JESUS SACRIFICES HIS SINLESS SELF FOR US

Two other men, both criminals and thieves, were led out with Him to be put to death.[143]

When they came to Golgotha, that is the Place of a Skull or Calvary, they gave Him vinegar mixed with myrrh and gall [a bitter and stupefying drug] to drink. But when He had tasted it, He would not drink any of it.[144]

There they crucified Him [hands and feet nailed to a wooden cross], along with the criminals; one on His right, the other on His left.[145] This fulfilled the Scripture [as God had prophesied through Isaiah about 700 years earlier] that says, "He was counted among the transgressors."[146]

> And what God had prophesied through David, about 1,000 years earlier, also came to pass: "They pierced My hands and My feet."[147]

It was the third hour [9:00 a.m.] when they crucified Him.[148]

JESUS FORGIVES THEM ALL

Then Jesus said, "Father, forgive them, for they do not know what they are doing."[149]

HE AGAIN IS MOCKED, DERIDED, AND TAUNTED

The people stood watching. They and the rulers with them derided Him, saying, "He saved others; let Him save Himself, if He is the Christ, the Messiah, the Chosen One of God."

The soldiers also mocked Him and, coming up to Him, said, "If you are the King of the Jews, save Yourself."

On the cross above Him was a sign written by Pilate, which read: "This is Jesus of Nazareth, the King of the Jews." Many of the Jews read this sign, for Jesus was crucified near the city, and the sign was written in Hebrew, Greek, and Latin.

Then the chief priests of the Jews went to Pilate and said, "Do not write, 'The King of the Jews' but 'He said, "I am King of the Jews."'"

Pilate answered, "What I have written, I have written."[150]

THE SOLDIERS GAMBLE FOR HIS CLOTHES

When the soldiers had crucified Jesus, they took His clothes and divided them into four parts, to every soldier a part, and gambled for them, to determine what each soldier would take.

They also took His cloak. Now the cloak was seamless, woven in one piece from top to bottom. So they said to themselves, "Don't tear it, but cast lots for it [similar to throwing dice], to determine who shall have it." This fulfilled the Scripture [as God had prophesied to the prophet David about 1,000 years earlier] that says, "They parted My clothing among them, and for My garment they cast lots."[151]

They sat down and watched Him, and the people stood looking at Him.[152]

Jesus Is Further Mocked, Reviled, and Ridiculed

Those who passed by verbally abused and reviled Him, shaking their heads and saying, "Oh, You Who destroy the temple and build it in three days, save Yourself and come down from the cross! If You are the Son of God, come down from the cross!"

The chief priests, mocking Him, with the scribes and elders, also said among themselves, "He saved others, but He cannot save Himself. If He is Christ, the Messiah, the King of Israel, let Him come down from the cross right now so that we may see it; then we will believe Him. He trusted in God; let God deliver Him now, if He wants Him, for He said, 'I am the Son of God.'"

The thieves who were crucified with Him also cast the same abuse at Him and reviled Him.[153]

He Provides Care for His Mother

Now by the cross of Jesus stood His mother and her sister, Mary the wife of Cleophas, and Mary Magdalene. When Jesus saw His mother and the disciple whom He loved [John] standing by, He said to His mother, "Woman, there is your son!" Then He said to John, "There is your mother!" And from that time, John took her into his own home.[154]

One Thief Repents and Is Forgiven

One of the criminals who hung there again reviled Him, saying, "If You are Christ, the Messiah, save Yourself and us."

But this time the other thief rebuked him, saying, "Do you not fear God? You are under the same condemnation, but we have been condemned justly, for we receive the due rewards of our actions. However, this Man has done nothing wrong."

Then he said to Jesus, "Lord, consider me when You come into Your kingdom."

"Believe Me," Jesus answered him, "you shall be with Me in paradise."[155]

Darkness Covers the Earth

At the sixth hour [noon], the sun was darkened. And there was darkness everywhere until the ninth hour [3:00 p.m.].[156]

CHAPTER EIGHT

JESUS—GOD'S ASTOUNDING SACRIFICE

About the ninth hour, Jesus cried out with a loud voice, "Eloi, Eloi, lama sabachthani?" which means, "My God, My God, why have you forsaken Me?"[157]

> *God had prophesied this through the prophet David about 1,000 years earlier.*[158]

Some of those who stood by, when they heard it, said, "Look, He calls for Elijah."

> *This must have been the moment when the Father placed on Jesus all the sin, guilt, and condemnation of the whole human race. God laid on Jesus the iniquity of us all and made Him Who knew no sin to be sin for us, so that we might become the righteousness of God in Him.*[159]
>
> *Up to this point, the Father must have been close to Jesus, enabling and strengthening Him all through this terrible ordeal. But now, suddenly, God had to completely break off the sweet, close intimacy and totally separate Himself from His dearly beloved Son. What an astounding and painful sacrifice this must have been for both the Father and the Son!*[160]

> *This is how greatly and intensely God loves every one of us and wants us to be forgiven, cleansed, and reconciled back into His astounding Father-love again!*

After this, Jesus, knowing that everything had been accomplished, in order that the Scripture might be fulfilled, said "I am thirsty." Now a vessel full of sour wine was there. So, someone ran and took a sponge and filled it with the vinegar [sour wine], put it on a pole, and put it to His mouth and gave Him a drink.[161]

The rest said, "Leave Him alone. Let us see whether Elijah will come to save Him and take Him down."[162]

JESUS GIVES UP HIS LIFE

When Jesus had drunk the vinegar, He shouted again with a loud voice, "It is finished."

Then He said, "Father, into Your hands I commit My spirit." Having said this, He bowed His head and gave up His spirit.[163]

WHY GOD SACRIFICED HIS OWN BELOVED SON

> *The following paraphrased Scriptures explain the reason for God's Astounding Sacrifice of His Son.*
>
> Jesus bore our sins in His Own body on the cross, so that we, having died to sins, might live for righteousness.[164] He bore the sins of many and made intercession for sinners.[165]
>
> For the wages of sin is death [both physical and spiritual], but the gift of God is eternal life through Jesus Christ our Lord.[166]

It is appointed for men to die once, but after this the judgment day.[167]

Death and hell were cast into the lake of fire. This is the second [spiritual] death. Anyone not found written in the Book of Life was cast into the lake of fire.[168]

God demonstrated His great, astounding love toward us in that, while we were still sinners, Christ died for us.[169] Christ suffered once for sins, the Just for the unjust, that He might bring us back and reconcile us to God.[170]

All we like sheep have gone astray; we have turned, every one, to his own way; and God laid on Jesus the iniquity of us all. He was wounded for our transgressions, He was bruised for our iniquities; the punishment for our peace was upon Him, and by His wounds we are healed.[171]

The Lord also made His soul an offering for our sin. Jesus Christ Himself is the payment of the penalty for our sins, and not for ours only but also for those of the whole world. He poured out His soul to death, to give us the gift of eternal life.[172]

Jesus' soul descended into the lower parts [the heart] of the earth [hell].[173]

God prophesied through David concerning Jesus, "You [God] will not leave My soul in hell, nor will You allow Your Holy One to experience decay."[174]

God's astounding love toward us was demonstrated in that God has sent His only begotten Son into the world, that we might live through Him. In this is love, not that we loved God, but that He loved us and sent His Son to be the payment for our sins.[175]

The Gospel of Christ, the proclaiming of the cross, is the power of God to salvation to everyone who believes.[176]

Thanks be to God for His incomparable gift.[177]

Jesus took the punishment for our sins on His body (physical death), and also took the punishment for our sins on His soul (spiritual death in hell). When He died, He committed His spirit to the Father, but His soul paid for our sins in the depths of hell, while His pierced and battered body lay for three days and three nights in that dark, cold tomb.

The Scriptures definitely state that Jesus' soul was in hell but do not describe Jesus' suffering and atonement for our sins in hell, likely because it is far beyond human comprehension.

Jesus Himself prophesied that "as Jonah was three days and three nights in the belly of the great fish [whale], so will the Son of Man be three days and three nights in the heart of the earth [hell]."[178]

THE EARTH QUAKES

Then there was an earthquake. The rocks split and the tombs were shaken open. And the veil of the temple was torn in two in the middle, from top to bottom.[179]

Now the centurion [a captain in charge of 100 Roman soldiers] who stood opposite Jesus and the guards who were with him saw that He shouted out like this and gave up His spirit and saw the earthquake and what was happening, and they were terrified. The centurion praised God, saying, "Certainly this was a righteous Man. Truly this Man was the Son of God."[180]

And all the people that came together to watch, seeing the things that were happening, beat their chests [an expression of sorrow and repentance], and returned to the city.[181]

Afar off, watching these things, stood Jesus' friends and the women who followed Him from Galilee and who ministered to Him, among whom was Mary Magdalene, Mary (the mother of James-the-Less and Joseph), Salome, the mother of Zebedee's children (James and John), and many other women who came up with Him to Jerusalem.[182]

Jesus' Side Is Pierced, and His Blood Pours Out

It was the [Sadducees'] Passover preparation day. So that the bodies would not remain on the cross on the Sabbath day (because that Sabbath was the [Sadducees'] Passover high Sabbath), the Jews asked Pilate to have their legs broken [to hasten their death] and that they might be taken away. Then the soldiers came and broke the legs of the one and then the other man who was crucified with Jesus.[183]

When they came to Jesus and saw that He was dead already, they did not break His legs; but one of the soldiers pierced His side with a spear, and immediately blood and water poured out. These things were done to fulfill the Scripture [prophesied by God through the prophet David about 1,000 years earlier]: "A bone of His shall not be broken."[184] And yet another Scripture [given through the prophet Zechariah about 500 years earlier] prophesied, "They shall look on Him Whom they pierced."[185]

The one who saw this [John] testifies, and his testimony is true, and he knows what he says is true, so that you who are reading this might believe.[186]

THE ASTOUNDING SHED BLOOD OF JESUS

The following paraphrased Scriptures explain the purpose and effect of God's Astounding Sacrifice.

We have redemption [salvation, buying us back from slavery] through Jesus' blood, the forgiveness of sins, according to the riches of His grace that He lavished on us.[187] He loved us and washed us from our sins in His own blood.[188] The shed blood of Jesus Christ, God's Son, cleanses us from all sin.[189]

Though our sins are like scarlet, they shall be white as snow; though they are red like crimson, they shall be white as wool.[190]

Wash me, and I shall be whiter than snow.[191]

Now, we are not our own, for we are bought with a price [the precious blood of Jesus]; therefore we should glorify God in our body and in our spirit, which belong to God.[192]

RECEIVING JESUS' ASTOUNDING SACRIFICE

Offer this to Jesus as your expression of love and gratitude for His Astounding Sacrifice.

I believe in Your sacrifice, redemption-all-complete,
Through Your blood, Lord Jesus Christ!
I receive Your salvation, forgiveness, gift-of-eternal-life,
Through Your precious shed blood, Lamb of God!

I accept Your cleansing, transforming, sin-destroying-power,
Through Your blood, Lord Jesus Christ!
I trust Your, authority, and wonder-working-power,
Through Your precious shed blood, Lamb of God!

I take Your total, supreme, devil-defeating-power,
Through Your blood, Lord Jesus Christ!
I claim Your conquest, triumph, victory-all-complete,
Through Your precious shed blood, Lamb of God!

I possess Your Holy Spirit's love-joy-and-peace,
Through Your blood, Lord Jesus Christ!
I enjoy access and bold entrance-to-Father's-throne,
Through Your precious shed blood, Lamb of God!

I give You my love, adoration, and deep-deep-gratitude,
For all that Your blood purchased for me, Lord Jesus Christ!
I offer You all my worship, praise, and glory-for-evermore,
For Your precious, victorious shed blood, Lamb of God!

I present complete dedication of my spirit-soul-and-body,
Unto You, my Shepherd, Redeemer, my Lord Jesus Christ!
I vow my will, my service, the surrender-of-my-all,
Unto You, my precious, glorious Savior, Lamb of God!

(By a redeemed sinner, now a forgiven, cleansed, transformed, and very grateful child of God—John G. Hutchinson)

JUDAS, HIS BETRAYER, HANGS HIMSELF

Judas, who had betrayed Him, became remorseful when he saw that Jesus was condemned. He brought the thirty pieces of silver back to the chief priests and elders, saying, "I have sinned by betraying innocent blood."

"What does that matter to us?" they answered. "That's your problem." So he threw down the pieces of silver in the temple and left.

The chief priests took the silver pieces and said, "It is not lawful to put them in the treasury, because it is the price of blood." They conferred among themselves and then used the silver, Judas' wage of iniquity, to buy the potter's field to use as a burial ground for foreigners. For that reason, that field was called the Field of Blood.

This fulfilled what God spoke by Jeremiah the prophet [about 600 years earlier]: "And they took the thirty pieces of silver, the price of Him Who was valued, Whom they of the children of Israel did value, and gave them for the potter's field, as the Lord had appointed."[193]

Then Judas went out and hanged himself, and falling headlong, he burst open in the middle, and all his intestines gushed out. And everyone who lived in Jerusalem heard about it.[194]

CHAPTER NINE

JESUS' BURIAL

JESUS' BURIAL IS ARRANGED

There was a rich man named Joseph, an honorable council member, a good and just man. He was a disciple of Jesus, but secretly, because he was afraid of the Jews. He had not agreed with the decision and actions of the Jewish council. He was from Arimathea, a city of the Jews. He also waited for the coming of the kingdom of God. Joseph went boldly to Pilate and asked that he might take away the body of Jesus, because it was the [Sadducees'] preparation day, that is, the day before [their Passover high] Sabbath, and evening was near [after which no work could be done].

Pilate was amazed that Jesus was already dead. He called for the centurion and asked him whether Jesus had been dead for very long. When Pilate heard the centurion's answer, he gave Joseph permission and commanded the body to be given to him.

So Joseph came and took down the body of Jesus. And Joseph bought fine linen. Nicodemus, who first came to Jesus by night, came also and brought about one hundred pounds of a mixture of myrrh and aloes [spices and perfumed oil used for embalming]. Then they took the body of Jesus and wrapped it in the clean linen cloths with the spices, following the burial practices of the Jews.

He Is Buried in a Borrowed Tomb

Now in the place where Jesus was crucified there was a garden; and in the garden was Joseph's own new tomb, which had been carved out of the rock, in which no one had ever yet been buried. They laid Jesus there, since the tomb was close by, because it was the [Sadducees'] preparation day. And they rolled a large stone over the door of the tomb. The women who came with Jesus from Galilee followed after them and saw the tomb and how His body was laid. And Mary Magdalene and the other Mary (the mother of Joseph), sitting opposite the tomb, saw where He was laid. Then they left, since the [Sadducees' Passover] high Sabbath approached.[195]

Jesus' Tomb Is Sealed and Guarded

Now the next day [the Sadducees' Passover high Sabbath], the day after their preparation day, the chief priests and Pharisees came altogether to Pilate, saying, "Sir, we remember that while He was yet alive that deceiver said, 'After three days I will rise again.' Therefore, command that the tomb be secured until after the third day, in case His disciples come by night, steal Him away, and say to the people, 'He is risen from the dead,' so the last mistake shall be worse than the first."

"You have your own [temple] guards," Pilate responded. "Go your way; make it as secure as you can." So they went and made the tomb secure, sealing the stone and setting their own Jewish guards.[196]

Three Women Prepare to Anoint Jesus' Body

The day after the [Sadducees' Passover high] Sabbath, Mary Magdalene, Mary (the mother of James), and Salome bought sweet spices to anoint Jesus. And the women who came with Him from Galilee prepared the spices and perfumed oils. Then they rested on the [regular] Sabbath day according to God's commandment.[197]

Chapter Ten

Jesus' Astounding Resurrection

God Raises Jesus from the Dead

God raised Jesus from the dead, as explained in the following paraphrased Scriptures. This must have occurred sometime after sunset, the end of the regular weekly Jewish Sabbath, very early on the first day of the week.

God, according to the exceeding greatness of His mighty power, raised Jesus Christ from the dead.[198]

God raised Him up and destroyed the sting of death, because it was not possible that He, the sinless Son of God, could be held by death.[199]

Through His death, Jesus annulled him who had the power of death, that is, the devil, and released those who through fear of death were all their lives subject to bondage.[200] He disarmed Satan's principalities and powers and made a public spectacle of them, triumphing over them [by His crucifixion and resurrection].[201]

Christ died, rose, and lived again that He might be Lord of both the dead and the living.[202]

Christ was raised from the dead by the glory of the Father in order to declare us righteous, so that we should

walk in newness of life, with a living hope, through His
resurrection.²⁰³

THE ANGEL OF THE LORD OPENS THE TOMB

There was a great earthquake, for the angel of the Lord came
down from heaven and rolled back the stone from the door
of the tomb and sat on it. His face was like lightning and his
clothing, white as snow. The guards trembled and fainted out of
fear, and then fled into the city.²⁰⁴

Many bodies of the righteous who had died arose and came
out of the graves after His resurrection. They went into the holy
city, Jerusalem, and appeared to many.²⁰⁵

THREE WOMEN COME TO ANOINT JESUS' BODY

While it was still dark, just as it began to dawn, Mary Magdalene,
the other Mary (the mother of James), and Salome came to the
tomb, bringing the sweet spices they had prepared to anoint
Jesus' body. They asked each other, "Who shall roll the stone
away from the door of the tomb for us?" for the stone was very
large. But when they looked, they saw that the stone was already
rolled away.²⁰⁶

When Mary Magdalene saw that Jesus' body was not there,
she immediately ran to Simon Peter and to John, the other
disciple whom Jesus loved.²⁰⁷

AN ANGEL PROCLAIMS, "HE IS RISEN!"

The other two women, entering into the tomb, saw a young
man sitting on the right side, clothed in a long white garment;

and they were frightened. The angel said to the women, "Don't be afraid. I know that you seek Jesus of Nazareth, Who was crucified. He is not here, for He is risen as He said He would. Come, see the place where the Lord lay. Now go quickly and tell His disciples and Peter that He is risen from the dead and goes before you into Galilee. You shall see Him there, as He said to you. Look, I have told you."

They went out quickly and fled from the tomb, trembling with fear and amazed with great joy. They ran to tell His disciples, but they said nothing to anyone else, for they were afraid.[208]

THE GUARDS REPORT TO THE CHIEF PRIESTS

Now while Mary (the mother of James) and Salome were going to tell the disciples, some of the guards came into the city and told the chief priests what had happened. When they were assembled with the elders and had taken counsel, they gave large sums of money to the soldiers, telling them, "Say, 'His disciples came by night and stole Him away while we slept.' If Pilate, the governor, finds out, we will convince him and protect you." So they took the money and did as they were told. So this story is commonly reported among the Jews until this day.[209]

PETER, JOHN, AND MARY MAGDALENE RUN TO JESUS' EMPTY TOMB

In the meantime, Mary Magdalene had come to Simon Peter and John. She told them, "They have taken the Lord out of the tomb, and we do not know where they have put Him."[210]

So Peter and John went out and ran together with Mary to the tomb. John outran Peter and arrived at the tomb first.

Stooping down and looking in, he saw the linen clothes lying there, but he did not go in.

Then Simon Peter, following him, arrived. He went into the tomb and saw the linen clothes lying by themselves and the cloth that had been wrapped around Jesus' head, not lying with the linen clothes but wrapped together in a place by itself. Then John, who had arrived at the tomb first, also went in; and he saw and believed. But they did not yet understand the Scripture that He would rise again from the dead. Then the two disciples went away again to their own place, Peter wondering in himself at what had happened.[211]

Jesus Shows Himself Alive to Mary Magdalene

But Mary Magdalene stood outside the tomb, crying. As she wept, she stooped down and looked into the tomb and saw two angels in white, one sitting at the head and the other sitting at the feet where the body of Jesus had lain. They asked her, "Woman, why are you crying?"

"Because they have taken away my Lord," she responded, "and I don't know where they have laid Him." When she had said this, she turned her head back and saw Jesus standing there, but she did not recognize Him.

"Woman, why are you weeping?" Jesus asked. "Whom do you seek?"

Thinking He was the gardener, she responded, "Sir, if You have carried Him from here, tell me where You have laid Him, and I will take Him away."

"Mary," Jesus said.

She whirled around and cried, "Rabboni!" which means "Master," and then she ran and embraced Him.

"Do not cling to Me," Jesus said, "for I have not yet ascended to My Father. But go to My brothers and tell them, 'I ascend to My Father and your Father, and to My God and your God.'"[212]

Thus when Jesus had risen, He appeared first to Mary Magdalene, out of whom He had cast seven demons.[213] She went to the disciples who had been with Him, as they mourned and wept, and told them that she had seen the Lord and that He had said these things to her. But when they had heard He was alive and had been seen by her, they did not believe it.[214]

He Also Shows Himself Alive to the Other Two Women

As the other two women, Mary (the mother of James) and Salome, went to tell His disciples what the angel had told them, Jesus met them, saying, "Greetings." They came to Him, held Him by the feet, and worshipped Him. Then Jesus said to them, "Don't be afraid. Go tell My brothers that they must go into Galilee, and they shall see Me there."[215]

Other Women Come to Anoint Jesus' Body

Other women who came with Him from Galilee also came to the tomb very early in the morning on the first day of the week, bringing the spices that they had prepared. They found the stone rolled away from the tomb. They entered it but did not find the body of the Lord Jesus.

While they were wondering about this, two men in shining garments appeared to them. They were afraid and fell on their faces. The angels said to them, "Why do you seek the living among the dead? He is not here; He is risen. Remember what

He said to you when He was still in Galilee: 'The Son of Man must be delivered into the hands of sinful men and be crucified, and after the third day rise again.'"

Then they remembered His words, and they returned from the tomb and told everything to the eleven and to everyone else.[216]

It was Mary Magdalene, Johanna, Mary (the mother of James), and other women who were with them who told these things to the apostles. But the women's words seemed to them like idle gossip, and they did not believe the women.[217]

JESUS SHOWS HIMSELF ALIVE TO PETER AND TO TWO OTHER DISCIPLES

Then the Lord appeared to Simon Peter.[218]

After that, He appeared in another form to two of them, as they walked that same day and went into the countryside to a village called Emmaus, which was sixty furlongs [about seven miles or twelve kilometers] from Jerusalem.

While they talked of everything that had happened and reasoned together, Jesus Himself drew near and walked with them. But their perception was obscured so that they did not recognize Him. He asked them, "What are you talking about together as you walk, and why are you are sad?"

One of them, whose name was Cleopas, answered, "You must be a newcomer to Jerusalem, since you don't know the things that have happened there the last few days."

"What things?" He asked.

"Concerning Jesus of Nazareth, Who was a Prophet, mighty in deed and word before God and all the people," they responded. "The chief priests and our rulers delivered Him to be condemned to death and have crucified Him. We trusted that He would redeem and liberate Israel; but now it is the third day after this happened.

"Certain women of our group, who were at the tomb early this morning, astonished us. They did not find His body, and so they came, saying that they had seen angels who said that He was alive.

"So some of us went to the tomb and found it was just as the women had said, but they did not see Him."

Then He said to them, "O foolish ones, and slow of heart to believe what the prophets have spoken. Ought not Christ, the Messiah, to have suffered these things and to enter into His glory?"

Then beginning at Moses and through all the prophets, He explained to them in all the Scriptures the things concerning Him. As they drew near to the village where they were going, Jesus acted as though He was continuing on. But they held Him back, saying, "Stay with us, for it is almost evening, the day is almost over."

So He went in to stay with them. As He sat at the meal with them, He took bread and blessed it, broke it, and gave to them. Then their eyes were opened and they recognized Him; but He vanished out of their sight.

Then they said to one another, "Did not our hearts burn within us while He talked with us on the road and explained the Scriptures to us?"

They got up immediately and returned to Jerusalem, and found the eleven and those who were gathered together with them.

Some of them said, "The Lord has risen indeed and has appeared to Simon Peter." So these two told what happened to them on the road and how He was recognized by them in breaking of bread. But the other disciples did not believe them.[219]

HE SHOWS HIMSELF ALIVE TO HIS APOSTLES THAT EVENING

That same evening they sat at a meal. The doors were locked for fear of the Jews. As they spoke, Jesus Himself stood among them and said to them, "Peace be to you."

But they were terrified, and thought they were seeing a ghost.

"Why are you troubled?" He asked them. "And why do these thoughts arise in your hearts? Look at My hands and My feet, that it is really Me. Touch Me and see, for a ghost does not have flesh and bones, as you see I have."

When He had said this, He showed them His hands, His feet, and His side. The disciples were glad when they realized it was the Lord. But He reproved them for their unbelief and hardness of heart, because they did not believe those who had seen Him after He had risen.

Then Jesus said to them again, "Peace be to you. Just as My Father has sent Me, I send you."

When He had said this, He breathed on them and said to them, "Receive the Holy Spirit. Whosoever sins against you, forgive them, and they will be forgiven; and whosoever sins against you and you do not forgive them, they will remain unforgiven."

Since they still could not believe it for joy and were still wondering, He asked them, "Do you have any food here?" So they gave Him a piece of broiled fish and a piece of a honeycomb, and He took it and ate before them.

"This is what I told you while I was still with you," He said. "Everything must be fulfilled that was written concerning Me in the Law of Moses, in the Prophets, and in the Psalms."

Then He opened their understanding so that they could understand the Scriptures. He told them, "For this reason it is written and it was necessary for Christ, the Messiah, to suffer and to rise from the dead after the third day, that repentance and forgiveness of sins should be preached in His name among all the nations, beginning at Jerusalem. You are witnesses of these things."[220]

Thomas, one of the twelve, called the Twin, was not with them when Jesus appeared. So, the other disciples told him later, "We have seen the Lord."

But he responded, "Unless I shall see the print of the nails in His hands, put my finger into the print of the nails, and thrust my hand into His side, I will not believe."[221]

Later, Jesus Shows Himself Alive to Thomas

Eight days later, His disciples were inside again with the doors locked, and Thomas was with them. Then Jesus came, stood among them, and said, "Peace be to you." Then He said to Thomas, "Put your finger into My hands and put your hand into My side; be not unbelieving, but believing."

Thomas responded, "My Lord and my God."

"Thomas, you have believed because you have seen Me," Jesus said. "Blessed are those who have not seen and yet have believed."

Jesus did many other signs in the presence of His disciples, which are not written in this book;[222] but these are written so that you might believe that Jesus is the Christ, the Messiah, the Son of God, and that believing you might have eternal life through His name.[223]

HE SHOWS HIMSELF ALIVE TO SEVEN DISCIPLES IN GALILEE

After this, Jesus showed Himself again to His disciples at the Sea of Tiberius [the Sea of Galilee] in this way.

Simon Peter, Thomas (called the Twin), Nathanael of Cana in Galilee, the sons of Zebedee (James and John), and two others of His disciples were together.

Simon Peter said to them, "I'm going fishing."

"We will go with you," they responded.

They went right out and boarded a ship, but that night they caught nothing.

In the morning, Jesus stood on the shore, but the disciples did not recognize Him. Then Jesus asked them, "Have you any food?"

"No," they answered.

So He told them, "Cast the net on the right side of the ship, and you shall find fish." So they cast, and suddenly there were so many fish they could not draw in the net.

John, the disciple whom Jesus loved, said to Peter, "It's the Lord!"

Now when Simon Peter heard that it was the Lord, he put on his fisherman's outer garment, which he had taken off, and he threw himself into the sea. The other disciples came in the little ship dragging the net full of fish, for they were only about two hundred cubits [about one hundred yards or ninety meters] from land.

As soon as they came to land, they saw a fire of coals there with fish lying on it, and bread. Jesus said to them, "Bring some of the fish that you have just caught."

Simon Peter went and drew the net to land, full of large fish, one hundred and fifty-three. Even though there were so many fish, the net did not break.

"Come and eat," Jesus invited them.

None of the disciples dared ask Him, "Who are you?" knowing that it was the Lord. So Jesus took bread and fish and gave it to them. This was the third time that Jesus showed Himself to His disciples after He had risen from the dead.[224]

JESUS COMMISSIONS PETER TO FEED HIS SHEEP

When they had eaten, Jesus asked Simon Peter, "Simon, son of John, do you love [Greek *agape,* meaning God-love] Me more than these?"

"Yes, Lord," Peter responded. "You know that I love [Greek *phileo,* meaning friendship-love] You."

"Feed My lambs," Jesus said.

Jesus asked him the second time, "Simon, son of John, do you love [*agape*] Me?"

"Yes, Lord," Peter responded. "You know that I love [*phileo*] You."

"Feed My sheep," Jesus said.

Jesus asked him the third time, "Simon, son of John, do you love [*phileo*] Me?"

Peter was grieved because this third time Jesus asked him, "Do you love [*phileo*] Me?" So he responded, "Lord, You know all things; You know that I love [*phileo*] You."

"Feed My sheep," Jesus said. "I tell you truly, when you were young, you dressed yourself and walked where you wanted; but when you are old, you will stretch out your hands and someone else will dress you and carry you where you don't want to go." He said this to indicate by what death Peter should glorify God. When He had spoken this, He said to him, "Follow Me."

Then Peter, turning around, saw John following them. (John was the disciple whom Jesus loved and who also leaned on His chest at the Passover supper and asked, "Lord, who is the one that betrays You?") Seeing him, Peter asked Jesus, "Lord, and what shall this man do?"

"If I will that he remains until I come back," Jesus responded, "what is that to you? You follow Me." Then this report circulated among the believers, that John would not die. However, Jesus did not say to him, "He shall not die" but "If I will that he remains until I come, what is that to you?"

This John is the disciple who testifies of these things and wrote these things [in the Gospel of John]; and we know that his testimony is true.[225]

JESUS MEETS WITH HIS DISCIPLES ON A MOUNTAIN

Then the eleven disciples went away to a mountain in Galilee where Jesus had appointed for them to meet Him. When they saw Him there, they worshipped Him. But some still doubted.[226]

HE SHOWS HIMSELF ALIVE TO MANY MORE PEOPLE

After this, He was seen by more than 500 believers at one time. After that, He was seen by James, and then by all the apostles. To them He showed Himself alive after His suffering by many convincing proofs, being seen by them for a period of forty days, speaking of the things regarding the kingdom of God and giving commandments to them through the Holy Spirit.[227]

Jesus Promises the Baptism with the Holy Spirit and Power

When He and the apostles whom He had chosen were together again in Jerusalem, He gave commandments to them through the Holy Spirit, saying, "Look, I send upon you the Promise of My Father, the Holy Spirit, as I have told you before. Do not leave, but wait in the city of Jerusalem until you are clothed with power from heaven. John [the Baptist] truly baptized with water, but you shall be baptized with the Holy Spirit not many days from now."[228]

He Commands Us to Tell the Good News to the Whole World

Jesus further commanded them, saying, "All power in heaven and on earth is given to Me. You go, therefore, into the entire world, and tell all nations the good news, which is Christ crucified, Christ risen, repentance, and the forgiveness of sins.[229] Tell every person, and make disciples. Baptize them in the name of the Father, the Son, and the Holy Spirit, and teach them to obey everything I have commanded you. He who believes and is baptized shall be saved, but he who does not believe shall be condemned. These signs shall be seen in those who believe: in My name they shall cast out demons; they shall speak with new languages; they shall take up serpents; if they drink any deadly thing, it shall not hurt them; and they shall lay hands on the sick, and they shall recover. Know that I will be with you always, even to the end of the age."[230]

WHAT EXACTLY IS THE AUTHENTIC GOSPEL OF JESUS?

What, exactly, is the good news that we are to proclaim to every person? The answer to this is very important, a matter of life and death—eternal life or eternal death!

Jesus told us that it is "necessary" that Christ crucified, Christ resurrected, repentance, and forgiveness of sins—the gospel—be proclaimed in His name to all nations.[231] As a "necessary" part of His Great Commission, He commanded that these four truths be proclaimed to every person:

1. Christ was crucified, paying for all our sin by His death, redeeming us with His shed blood from the penalty and power of sin, and saving us from eternal hell.

2. Christ was resurrected and exalted far above all, for our total forgiveness, our complete acceptance, our transformation, and the gift of eternal life with God.

3. "Repentance" means to turn our hearts away from sin and self-centeredness and turn back to God, to obey Him, and to wholeheartedly follow Jesus as Lord and Savior.

4. Forgiveness of sins comes by receiving (believing in, trusting in) Jesus and His crucifixion as the complete sacrifice for our forgiveness and for the free imputing (crediting) to us of His perfect righteousness.

God says that this gospel of Christ, *the message of the cross,* is the power of God to salvation for everyone who believes.[232] But the proclamation of the gospel must be complete, having all the four "necessary" elements, in order to be "the power of God unto salvation." The apostle Paul said,

- "I have *fully* proclaimed the gospel of Christ."[233]
- "So that through me the message might be *fully* proclaimed."[234]

This is so important that God issues a very serious warning in Paul's letter to the Galatians: "I marvel that you are turning away…to a *different* gospel, which is *not another [gospel]*; but there are some who…want to *pervert* [distort] the gospel of Christ. But even if we, or an angel from heaven, preach *any other gospel* to you than what we have preached to you, let him be accursed [rejected, banned, excommunicated]."[235]

Satan knows that the original, "necessary," undiluted gospel defeats him and that it breaks his hold on his prisoners and transfers them into Christ's kingdom forever. So, Satan is constantly and subtly working to dilute, pollute, alter, twist, sugarcoat, weaken, and mutilate the authentic gospel. This is why God gave us the very serious warning in Paul's letter to the Galatians.

Not all of what is proclaimed today is the complete, authentic good news that Jesus commanded us to preach to all people. Some of it lacks "the power of God unto salvation." Nowhere in Scripture is there any instruction to make, or any example of making, the gospel "seeker-sensitive," "user-friendly" or "attractional." These approaches may make sense to human wisdom, but it is *not* God's wisdom.[236] We must communicate to people in the context of their culture, but we must *never* change the message. We must lovingly, humbly, and considerately present the complete gospel to unbelievers. But we *must not* water it down or leave out any of the four necessary elements to try to please people and make it more attractive to them, in order to induce a response.

The power of the original, necessary, undiluted gospel is consistently demonstrated all through the book of Acts and the rest of the New Testament. Here are just a few of many examples:

- On the day of Pentecost, in the power of the Holy Spirit, Peter preached Jesus crucified, Jesus resurrected and exalted, repentance, and the forgiveness of sins. And 3,000 people received Jesus and were baptized![237]

- Another time, Peter preached, "Repent, then, and turn to God, so that your sins may be wiped out."[238] And about 5,000 people received Jesus![239]

- "Nor is there salvation in any other, for there is no other name under heaven given among men by which we must be saved."[240]

- "God…raised up Jesus whom you murdered by hanging on a tree [cross]. Him God has exalted to His right hand to be Prince [King] and Savior, to give repentance…and forgiveness of sins."[241]

The apostle Paul tells us that the gospel he always preached—"Christ crucified"—includes Christ resurrected and exalted. These are all one inseparable package: "We preach Christ crucified…the power of God and the wisdom of God."[242]

- "For I resolved to know nothing while I was with you except Jesus Christ and him crucified."[243]

- "I declare to you the gospel…that Christ died for our sins according to the Scriptures, and that He was buried, and that He arose again the third day according to the Scriptures."[244]

- "You know that I have not hesitated to preach anything that would be helpful to you but have taught you publicly and from house to house...that [you] must turn to God in repentance and have faith in our Lord Jesus."[245]

- "Jesus Christ was clearly portrayed among you as crucified."[246]

Chapter Eleven

Jesus' Astounding Ascension

Jesus Ascends Back into Heaven

Then He led them out as far as to Bethany, to the Mount of Olives, which is a Sabbath day's journey [just over half a mile, or about 900 meters] from Jerusalem. When they came together they asked Him, "Lord, will You restore the kingdom to Israel now?"

"You are not entitled to know the times or the seasons that the Father has under His own power," He answered. "But you shall receive power after the Holy Spirit comes on you; and you shall be witnesses to Me in Jerusalem, in all Judea, in Samaria, and to the ends of the earth."[247]

When He had said this, He lifted up His hands and blessed them. As He blessed them, they saw him being separated from them and taken up into heaven, and He went into a cloud, out of their sight.[248]

While they looked intently towards heaven as He went up, two men in white clothing suddenly stood by them. The men said, "Galileans, why are you standing there, gazing up into heaven? This same Jesus, Who is taken up from you into heaven, shall come back in the same way as you have seen Him go into heaven."[249]

The Exalted Position of the Ascended Jesus

The following paraphrased Scriptures further explain the results of Jesus' crucifixion, burial, resurrection, and ascension.

Jesus, the author and finisher of our faith, for the joy that was set before Him, endured the cross, despising the shame.[250] When He had by His death purged our sins, He ascended into heaven.[251]

Then God seated Him at His own right hand and crowned Him with glory and honor.[252]

We now have a great High Priest Who has ascended into heaven, Jesus the Son of God, Who lives forever to intercede for us.[253] When He ascended up on high, He led captivity captive and gave gifts to men. He that descended is the One Who ascended far above all heavens, that He might fill all things.[254]

God has highly exalted Him far above all authority, power, might, and dominion and has given Him a position with authority that is above every name that is named, that at the name of Jesus every knee should bow, in heaven, on earth, and under the earth, not only in this world but also in that which is to come, and that every tongue should confess that Jesus Christ is Lord, to the glory of God the Father.[255]

God exalted Him to be King and Savior, both Lord and Christ, to give repentance and forgiveness of sins.[256]

Jesus received from God the Promise of the Father—which is the baptism, power, and fullness of the Holy Spirit—to pour out upon His disciples and upon all believers worldwide.[257]

The Lord said to Jesus, "Sit at My right hand, until I make Your enemies Your footstool."[258] God gave Jesus to be the head over all things.[259] For He must reign until He has put all enemies under His feet, and the last enemy that shall be destroyed is death.[260]

His Disciples Worship, Rejoice, and Pray with Expectancy

So they worshipped Him, and returned to Jerusalem with great joy. When they had entered the city, they went into an upper room, where Peter, James, John, Andrew, Philip, Thomas, Bartholomew, Matthew, James (the son of Alphaeus), Simon the Zealot, and Judas (the son of James) were staying.[261]

They remained unified in prayer with the women, Mary (the mother of Jesus), and the brothers of Jesus. They were also continually in the temple, praising and blessing God.[262]

CHAPTER TWELVE

JESUS DESIRES EVERYONE TO RECEIVE HIS SACRIFICE

The following paraphrased Scriptures explain the opportunity for relationship with God that is available to each of us as a result of Jesus' Astounding Sacrifice.

God says, "I so greatly and intensely love the whole human race that I gave and sacrificed My only Son, that whoever believes in Him should not perish but have everlasting life. For I did not send My Son into the world to condemn the world but that the world though Him might be saved. He that believes on Him, Jesus, is not condemned; but he who does not believe is condemned already, because he has not believed in the name of the only Son of God."[263]

Jesus says, "Look, I stand at the door of your heart and knock. If anyone hears My voice and opens the door, I will come in to them by My Spirit and we will feast together."[264]

God says, "As many as receive Jesus, who believe in Him, to them I give the right to become the children of God; who are born spiritually, not of blood, nor of the will of the flesh, nor of the will of man, but of My Spirit."[265]

How to Receive Jesus and His Great Salvation

Jesus commanded us not only to proclaim the complete "necessary" gospel; He *also commanded us to make disciples.* We are to lovingly, humbly, and patiently invite and urge people to turn to God, personally receive the crucified and resurrected Jesus as their Savior and Lord, and then follow and obey Him. Here is a guideline to help you lead people to personally receive Jesus.

- The gospel faces everyone with a decision: to obey *or* not to obey, to accept *or* to reject.
- "I have set before you life and death, blessing and cursing; therefore *choose life.*"[266] "And this is his command: to believe in the name of his Son, Jesus Christ."[267] This is *not* merely mental assent but a sincere, wholehearted decision to make that choice.
- To obey the gospel, we must take the following simple heart-actions that God commands: repent in our hearts, believe in Jesus, receive Jesus, open up to Jesus, and begin to follow Jesus.

A. Repent in your heart, which means turn your heart back to God and give yourself to Him.[268]

- Ask God to give you the will and the power to turn to Him and to change. Repentance is a gift from Him, to those who choose it and ask Him for it. It is *His* power that changes you, *not* yours. This is very good news!
- "The Lord is…not willing that any should perish but that *all* should come to *repentance.*"[269]

B. Believe in Jesus, in His death for your sins, and His resurrection for your new life, for "whoever believes in him [Jesus] shall not perish but have eternal life."[270]

• The Greek word translated "believe in" or "believe on" means to *trust* in, *rely* on, *depend* upon. It is much more than just mental assent, and more than just believing that He exists. "Believing in" is a decision, a choice, an act of your will, to *trust* in Jesus for your salvation.

• If you really "believe in" Jesus, you *will* act on it, receive Him and His wonderful gift of eternal life, and commit yourself and your salvation to Him.

C. Receive Jesus, person-to-Person, by simple child-like faith.[271]

• "For it is by grace you have been saved, through faith— and this [faith] not from yourselves, it is the *gift of God*—not by works, so that no one can boast."[272] This, too, is good news! God will give you faith if you really want to be saved.

• "But as many as *received Him* [Jesus], to them He gave the right to become children of God, to those who believe in His name: who were born…of God."[273]

D. Open up to Jesus and invite Him to come in.

• He will not force His way into your life. You must open your heart to Him!

• "Behold, I stand at the door and knock. If anyone hears My voice and *opens the door,* I will come in to him and dine [feast] with him, and he with Me."[274] He promises to do this!

- Swing *wide open* the door of your heart, your will, and your life, and ask Him to come in. Choose to receive Jesus as your Savior *and* as your Lord. He will be absolutely faithful to come into you, by His Spirit, to make you a new person. As you receive Him, *give yourself* to Him, thus entering into a mutual love relationship with Him.
- *Ask Him* to come in. "That if you *confess* with your mouth, 'Jesus is Lord,' and believe in your heart that God raised him from the dead, you *will be saved*"[275]— from a lost eternity. Say it to Him out loud, even if you are alone. This will be recorded in heaven, in the Book of Life. Jesus' Spirit will unite with your spirit, and you will be born anew, spiritually: the beginning of you as a new person!
- *Ask Him also* to fill (baptize, immerse) you to overflowing with His Holy Spirit. This, too, is His promise for you![276] "But you will receive power when the Holy Spirit comes on you; and you will be my witnesses."[277] Then, with His power and His love filling you, invite other people to receive Jesus Christ.

E. Begin to follow Jesus, out of love and gratitude for His great love and salvation.
- "We love Him because He first loved us."[278]
- Jesus said, "If you love me, you will obey what I command."[279]
- This is the out-working of your repentance. It is denying your old self, not saving your life for yourself but giving your life to Jesus for His purposes and His will and for your own eternal rewards.[280]

- "You are not your own…For you were bought at a price [the shed blood of Jesus]; therefore *glorify* God in your body and in your spirit, which are God's."[281]

A PRAYER TO RECEIVE JESUS

Feel very free to use these words or say these things to God in your own words, from deep inside your heart. God will surely hear and eagerly answer when you pray this sincerely.

God, I thank You for Your great eternal, Astounding Love for me that compelled You to make the Astounding Sacrifice of Your dearly beloved Son, Jesus Christ, to pay the penalty for all my sin and to reconcile me back to You.

Heavenly Father, I need Your great love, and I need Jesus' great redemption. I have sinned, and I need Your forgiveness and cleansing. Please forgive me. I give myself to You. Give me the will and the power to repent: to turn to You and change my ways.

Father, give me the simple childlike faith to receive, personally, Your Astounding Love for me and to receive Jesus' Astounding Sacrifice as Your free gift for my eternal salvation.

God, right now, by faith, I receive Your great love for me and Your wonderful gift of eternal life through Jesus' crucifixion, resurrection, and ascension. I thank You with all my heart.

Jesus, right now, by faith, I receive You as my Creator and my crucified, risen, ascended Savior. And I receive Your crucifixion, resurrection, and ascension for my forgiveness and my salvation. I thank You with all my heart.

Jesus, I open my heart and life to You. Come into my life as my Savior and my Lord, and begin to make me a new person, the person I was meant to be. Give me the power to love You and to live for You, not by my power, but by the great power of Your resurrection.

Jesus, fill me to overflowing with Your life and Your Spirit. I receive Your promise of the Holy Spirit. I trust You to do this. I thank You very much with all my heart.

CHAPTER THIRTEEN

JESUS POURS OUT THE PROMISE OF THE FATHER

JESUS' BETRAYER IS REPLACED

In those days, Peter stood up in the midst of the disciples (there were about one hundred and twenty of them) and said, "Brothers and sisters, this Scripture needs to be fulfilled, which the Holy Spirit spoke before by the prophet David concerning Judas, who acted as guide to those who arrested Jesus; he was included with us and was part of this ministry.[282]

"For it is written in the book of Psalms, 'Let his house be desolate, and let no man dwell in it.'[283] And it is also written, 'Let another take his position.'[284] Therefore, one of the men who have been with us throughout the time that the Lord Jesus was with us, beginning from the baptism of John until the day that He was taken up from us, must be appointed to be a witness with us of His resurrection."[285]

So they nominated two: Joseph called Barsabas, who was surnamed Justus, and Matthias. They prayed, "Lord, You know the hearts of all men; show which of these two You have chosen, that he may become part of this ministry and apostleship from which Judas fell because of sin, that he might go to his own place." Then they cast their lots [similar to throwing dice].

The lot was for Matthias, so he was numbered with the eleven apostles.[286]

When the day of Pentecost [Jewish Feast of First Fruits, or Harvest] arrived [fifty days after the Passover high Sabbath], they were all together with one accord in one place. Suddenly there came a sound from heaven like a rushing mighty wind, which completely filled the house where they were sitting. Individual flames like fire appeared to them; a flame sat on each of them. And they were all filled with the Holy Spirit and began to speak in other languages as the Spirit enabled them.

There were staying in Jerusalem devout Jews from many nations. Now when this noise was heard, a crowd came together. They were astounded because every man heard the disciples speak in his own language. And they were all amazed and marveled, saying to one another, "Look, are not these people Galileans? So how do we all hear them in our own language, our mother tongue? Parthians, Medes, Elamites, those who live in Mesopotamia, in Judea and Cappadocia, in Pontus, Asia, Phrygia, and Pamphylia, in Egypt, in the parts of Libya about Cyrene, foreigners from Rome, Jews and proselytes [Gentile converts to Judaism], Cretes and Arabians—we hear them speak in our languages about the wonderful works of God."

So they were all amazed and wondered, saying to one another, "What does this mean?" Others, mocking, said, "These men are full of new wine."[287]

THE HOLY SPIRIT SPEAKS THROUGH PETER

Peter, standing up with the eleven, called out to them, "You men of Judea and all who are staying in Jerusalem, listen to my words and understand. These people are not drunk, as you think, since it is only the third hour of the day [9:00 a.m.]. Rather, this is what was prophesied by the prophet Joel:[288] 'In the last days, says God, I will pour out My Spirit on all flesh; your sons and your daughters shall prophesy, your young men shall see visions, and your old men shall dream dreams. I will pour out My Spirit on My male and female servants in those days, and they shall prophesy. And I will show wonders in heaven above, and signs in the earth beneath: blood, fire, and smoke. The sun shall be turned into darkness and the moon into blood, before the great and notable day of the Lord comes. And whoever shall call on the name of the Lord shall be saved.'[289]

"You men of Israel, listen to me: Jesus of Nazareth was a man among you Who was approved of God by miracles, wonders, and signs, which God did by Him in your midst, as you yourselves also know. Being delivered up by the predetermined counsel and foreknowledge of God, you have taken Him, and by wicked hands you have crucified and killed Him. God has raised Him up, having released the cords of death, because He could not be held by it. For David spoke concerning Him:[290] 'I foresaw the Lord always before my face, because He is on my right hand, that I should not be shaken. Therefore my heart rejoiced, and my tongue was glad; also my body shall rest in hope, because You will not leave My soul in hell, neither will You allow Your Holy One to experience decay. You have made known to Me the ways of life; You shall make Me full of joy in Your presence.'[291]

"Brothers and sisters, let me speak freely to you of our forefather David, who is both dead and buried and whose tomb is with us to this day. He was a prophet, and knew that God had made an oath to him that from his earthly descendants, He would raise up Christ to sit on His throne. Foreseeing this,

David spoke of the resurrection of Christ, that His soul was not left in hell; neither did His body decay.

"This Jesus, God has raised up; all of us are witnesses to it. Therefore having been exalted by the right hand of God and having received of the Father the promise of the Holy Spirit, He has poured out what you now see and hear. David has not ascended into the heavens, but he himself says,[292] 'The LORD said to my Lord, "Sit on My right hand, until I make Your enemies Your footstool."'[293]

"Therefore let all the house of Israel know for certain that God has made Jesus, Whom you have crucified, both Lord and Christ, the Messiah."[294]

The Holy Spirit Gives Great Conviction and Repentance

Now when they heard this, they were pierced to the heart and asked Peter and the rest of the apostles, "Brothers, what shall we do?"

Peter responded, "Every one of you must repent and be baptized in the name of Jesus Christ for the forgiveness of sins, and you shall receive the gift of the Holy Spirit. For the promise is for you and your children, and for all who are in the world, as many as the Lord our God shall call."

Then with many other words he testified and urged them, saying, "Save yourselves from the perverse mind-set of the world."

Those who gladly received what he said were baptized, and that very day about three thousand were added to the number of disciples.[295]

The Holy Spirit Gives Great Love, Joy, Unity, and Many Miracles

And they continued faithfully in the apostles' teachings and fellowship, in breaking of bread, and in prayers. Awe came upon every soul, and many wonders and miracles were done by the apostles.

All who believed were together and shared everything together. They sold their possessions and goods and gave them away, as anyone had need.

Continuing daily with one accord in the temple and breaking bread from house to house, they ate their meals with gladness and undivided hearts, praising God and having favor with all the people. And the Lord added to the disciples those who were being saved every day.[296]

Jesus' Church Spreads Across the World

They went out and preached everywhere, the Lord working with them and confirming His word with signs and miracles.[297]

> *Read "the rest of the story" in Acts chapters 3 to 28 and the rest of the New Testament.*

Chapter Fourteen

Jesus—God's Astounding Love-Gift Sacrifice

> *Offer this to God, with deep gratitude and worship, as your love-gift to Him, for His astounding Love-Gift to you.*

Jesus, You Sacrificed Your Sinless Self—for Us

Heavenly Father, Your great Astounding Love
Moved You to create us as Your Own dear children!
But we have sinned against You and terribly disobeyed You.
But You still totally love us and still intensely desire us!
And You manifested Yourself to us as a Man—Jesus!
"Great is the mystery": "The Word became flesh" to live
And to die, to give forgiveness and eternal life—to us all!

Jesus, You are indeed The Only Son of God,
Full of God's boundless love, grace and truth.
Truly You are God Manifest in the Flesh for me—
And for Your whole dark, sinful, lost world!
Jesus, all of God's glory shone from Your sinless life;
And Your crucifixion was God's Astounding Sacrifice,
To give His white-hot-burning Father-Love—to us all!

Jesus, in that garden, You prayed alone in extreme agony.
With vehement cries, tears, and sweat like drops of blood,
You faced the terrible price of paying for human sin,
Yes, for all the sins of human history—for us all!
Jesus, Your sinless soul recoiled from the shame and pain
Of bearing all the vileness and evil of mankind! But You
Obeyed the Father's will, to give salvation—to us all!

Jesus, You were betrayed, denied, and utterly forsaken,
Spit on, brutally bruised, and cruelly beaten,
Rejected, slandered, condemned, and crucified,
Yes, for me—and yes, for us all!
Jesus, You willingly paid the greatest price:
You were God's great Love-Gift Sacrifice,
On Your cruel, cruel cross, for me—and for us all!

Jesus, King of Glory, You were horribly humiliated,
Reviled, ridiculed, mocked, shamed, and scorned!
You were stripped, whipped, then terribly blasphemed,
For me—and for us all!
Jesus, You paid the terribly painful price:
Your shed blood was God's precious sacrifice,
On Your cruel, cruel cross, for me—and for us all!

Jesus, You willingly endured the whip, the thorns, the nails,
And Your back was like a fresh-plowed field.
Jesus, You then hung, nailed, for six long, torturous hours,
For me—and for us all!
Jesus, Your "appearance was marred more than any man."
A spear pierced Your heart, and blood and water flowed out,
On Your cruel, cruel cross, for me—and for us all!

Jesus, on Your cruel, cruel cross, You lovingly
Bore all our awful sin and all our great guilt!
You suffered, bled, and died there for me,
Even for me—and even for us all!
Jesus, You paid the full and complete price:
You were God's loving, ultimate sacrifice,
On Your cruel, cruel cross, for me—and for us all!

Then, Your pierced, battered body lay in that dark, cold tomb,
While Your spotless soul atoned for all our sin,
Suffering unimaginable horrors, in the depths of hell,
For me—and for us all!
Jesus, You paid the astounding, supreme price:
Your sinless soul was God's great "burnt sacrifice",
In the awful depths of hell, for me—and for us all!

Father, You Sacrificed
Your Dearly Beloved Son—for Us

Father, Your burning, immeasurable Father-Love for us all,
Compelled You, from the foundation of the world,
To plan and ordain all of Jesus' suffering and death,
For me—and for us all!
Father, You fully gave Yourself to us, through Jesus,
And He took all our sin, our death, and our hell,
On His cruel cross, and in His cold tomb—for us all!

Father, You were in Your Dearly Beloved Son,
Suffering fully as much as He,
To reconcile, to Yourself, Your whole lost world,
Including me—and including us all!

Jesus, through His crucifixion, is the only way back into
The welcoming arms of Your astounding, eternal Father-Love,
Through His cruel cross and His suffering in hell—for us all!

Father, You had to forsake Your Own Precious Son,
When You laid our iniquity upon Him, Your Holy One.
You made Jesus "to be sin for us" all,
Yes, for us all—including me!
Father, You paid the astounding, ultimate price:
Jesus, Himself, was Your precious Love-Gift Sacrifice,
On His cruel, cruel cross, for me—and for us all!

Father, the deep, deep anguish You must have felt,
To make Your Very Beloved Son, Jesus, suffer so,
To do all this to Your precious Only Son,
For me—and for us all!
Father, You paid the full atonement price:
Your Dear Son is Your supreme Love-Gift Sacrifice,
On His cruel—**but**—conquering cross—for us all!

FATHER, YOU SACRIFICED
YOUR PRECIOUS JESUS—FOR US ALL

For every man and woman, and
For every boy and girl,
Of every nation, tribe, and tongue,
On—all this planet Earth,
Jesus, You fully paid the everlasting price:
Redemption for Your whole human race,
On Your glorious, saving cross—for all the world!

Jesus, You defeated Satan and our old sinful natures!
You triumphantly won the keys to death and hell!
You overcame all the darkness of Your lost world,
For me—and for us all!
Jesus, You conquered all the demonic powers,
And became the King of kings and the Lord of lords,
Through Your victorious, triumphant cross—for us all!

How extremely precious each one of us must be to You,
Of what high, high value and great, great worth,
For You to make such an incredible sacrifice,
For me—and yes, for us all!
Jesus, we were all captives of Satan, sin, and selfishness;
And You totally paid the immense ransom-price,
On Your redeeming, liberating cross—for us all!

Jesus, You looked ahead to totally undeserving me,
And to all who would ever believe in and receive You.
You saw that our love would be a greatly cherished joy,
To You, Jesus—and also to You, Father,
A very precious treasure and an extreme delight,
And worth all of Your wonderful, substitutionary sacrifice,
On Your astounding, marvelous cross—for us all!

JESUS, FATHER, I NOW GRATEFULLY RECEIVE—YOU

Jesus, Father, I'm filled with great awe and wonder,
Totally astounded and absolutely amazed,
To see Your great, burning, eternal Father-Love for me—
And for Your whole, dark, sinful, lost world!
Jesus, Your passionate Love has totally won my heart,

By Your atoning and substitutionary death,
On Your precious, loving cross—for us all!

Jesus, spotless Passover Lamb of God,
By faith I receive You and Your precious shed blood.
I receive all of Your supreme, loving sacrifice.
And You want us—all by faith, to receive You!
Jesus, Father, fervent love and gratitude fill my heart,
And joyous praise overflows from my lips,
Because Your shed blood is the **River of Life**—for us all!

By Your death and resurrection, "all my sins are forgiven,"
Totally "blotted out," "never to be remembered,"
And they are all forever "cast into the depths of the sea."
And this is for—all who humbly receive You!
Jesus, instead of all my shameful sin, You now freely
Clothe me with all of Your glorious pure righteousness,
Through Your amazing, grace-filled cross—for us all!

Now, Jesus, You are seated on the highest throne in Heaven,
Risen, absolutely triumphant, from the dead!
You reign supreme, in all power and majesty,
Now and forever, for—all who have received You!
Jesus, You live victoriously, to intercede for us.
I now daily receive, by Your grace, Your total victory,
That flows from Your glorious throne—for us all!

JESUS, FATHER, I NOW TOTALLY GIVE MYSELF—TO YOU

Father, You love to choose and use us,
Especially the foolish and the weak,

Filling, and flowing out through even me,
And through—all who have received You!
Jesus, You live victoriously in my heart,
And Your Holy Spirit is now entwined with mine.
So, reveal Yourself to Your dark, lost world—through me!

Jesus, Father, I completely give You all of myself,
Fervently and joyfully, as a "living sacrifice."
This is my love-gift, with deep, deep gratitude,
To You, Jesus—and also to You, Father!
I totally dedicate and submit my all to You,
And I passionately apply to my whole life:
Your Cross. It is the **Tree of Life**, giving to me—
And to all who,
   By faith, sincerely
      Receive You, Jesus,
         As their Savior
           And as their Lord:
   Total forgiveness!
    Joyous welcome!
      Complete acceptance!
      Spiritual new birth!
        Great transformation!
         And Glorious **Eternal Life**!
Postscript:
   to be continued,
     exuberantly and passionately,
       throughout all of eternity!

*(By a redeemed sinner, now a forgiven, cleansed, transformed,
and very grateful child of God—John G. Hutchinson)*

ENDNOTES

1. Genesis 1:26–27.
2. Genesis 2:7.
3. 1 John 4:8, 16.
4. Genesis 3:21.
5. John 1:29.
6. Hebrews 9:11–15.
7. John 1:14; Philippians 2:5–8.
8. Colossians 1:19; Colossians 2:9.
9. 1 Timothy 3:16.
10. 1 John 2:2.
11. Genesis 1:1; John 1:1; Revelation 19:13.
12. John 1:3–4.
13. Galatians 4:4–5.
14. Luke 1:26–27, 31–32, 35.
15. Matthew 1:22–23. See Isaiah 7:14.
16. Isaiah 9:6.
17. John 1:14.
18. 1 John 1:1–3.
19. 1 Timothy 3:16.
20. Colossians 1:19; Colossians 2:9.
21. Philippians 2:6–8.

22. Hebrews 2:6–7, 9, 14–15; Galatians 1:4.

23. Romans 5:8.

24. John 3:16–17.

25. 1 Peter 1:18–20; Revelation 13:8; John 1:29.

26. Matthew 16:13–17; Mark 8:27–30; Luke 9:18–20.

27. Matthew 16:21; Mark 8:31; Luke 9:22.

28. Matthew 17:22–23; Mark 9:30–32; Luke 9:44–45, 51.

29. Mark 10:32–34; Luke 18:31–34.

30. John 12:1–8.

31. Matthew 21:1–3, 6–7; Mark 11:1–7; Luke 19:29–35; John 12:14.

32. Matthew 21:4–5; John 12:15. See Zechariah 9:9.

33. Matthew 21:8–9; Mark 11:8–10; Luke 19:36; John 12:12–13.

34. Luke 19:37–41.

35. Matthew 21:10–11.

36. John 12:19.

37. Mark 11:11.

38. Isaiah 56:7; Jeremiah 7:11.

39. Matthew 21:12–13; Mark 11:12, 15–18; Luke 19:45–46.

40. Matthew 21:14–15; Mark 11:18.

41. Matthew 21:17; Mark 11:19.

42. Matthew 21:18; Mark 11:27; Luke 19:47–48.

43. Matthew 21:23–27; Mark 11:27–33; Luke 20:1–8.

44. Matthew 21:45–46; Mark 12:12; Luke 20:19.

45. Luke 20:20; Mark 12:12.

46. John 12:31–33.

47. Matthew 26:1–2; Luke 22:1.

48. Matthew 26:3–5; Mark 14:1–2; Luke 22:2.

49. Matthew 26:6–13; Mark 14:3–9.

50. Zechariah 11:12.

51. Matthew 26:14–16; Mark 14:10–11; Luke 22:3–6.
52. Luke 21:37–38.
53. John 12:44–50.
54. Exodus 20:3–17.
55. Genesis 1:1–2:3.
56. For the origin and meaning of this festival, see Exodus 12:1–42 and Leviticus 23:1–8.
57. Exodus 12:14–16.
58. Exodus 12:2–13.
59. John 1:29; 1 Corinthians 5:7.
60. Matthew 26:17–19; Mark 14:12–16; Luke 22:7–13.
61. John 13:1.
62. Matthew 26:20; Mark 14:17; Luke 22:14–16.
63. 1 Corinthians 5:7.
64. Matthew 26:21; Mark 14:18; Luke 22:21.
65. Matthew 26:22–24; Mark 14:19–21; Luke 22:22–23.
66. Matthew 26:25.
67. Matthew 26:26–29; Mark 14:22–25; Luke 22:17–20. The apostle Paul also recounts this story in 1 Corinthians 11:23–26, which is where Jesus' command to drink the cup in remembrance of Him appears.
68. Luke 22:24–30.
69. John 13:2–11.
70. John 13:12–17.
71. See Psalm 41:9.
72. John 13:18–30.
73. John 13:31–35.
74. John 13:36–38; Mark 14:72.
75. John 14:1–14.
76. John 14:15–21.
77. John 14:22–31.

78. Luke 22:31–34; Mark 14:72.
79. Isaiah 53:12.
80. Luke 22:35–39.
81. Matthew 26:30; Mark 14:26; Luke 22:39; John 14:31.
82. John 15:1–17.
83. John 15:18–25. See Psalm 69:4.
84. John 15:26–27.
85. John 16:1–15.
86. John 16:16–33.
87. See Zechariah 13:7.
88. Matthew 26:31–35; Mark 14:27–31.
89. See for example Psalm 41:9.
90. John 17:1–26.
91. Matthew 26:36; Mark 14:32; Luke 22:39; John 18:1–2.
92. Matthew 26:36–38; Mark 14:32–34; Luke 22:40.
93. Matthew 26:39–44; Mark 14:35–40; Luke 22:41–44.
94. Matthew 26:45–46; Mark 14:41–42; Luke 22:45–46.
95. Matthew 26:47–50; Mark 14:43–45; Luke 22:47–48; John 18:3–4.
96. John 17:12. Specifically, Jesus said that He lost none of those God gave him except His betrayer, Judas.
97. John 18:5–9.
98. Matthew 26:50; Mark 14:46.
99. One legion is 3,000 to 6,000 soldiers.
100. See for example Isaiah 50:6 and Isaiah 53:7.
101. Matthew 26:51–54; Mark 14:47; Luke 22:49–51; John 18:10–11.
102. Matthew 26:55–56; Mark 14:48–49; Luke 22:52–53. See for example Isaiah 50:6 and Isaiah 53:7.
103. Matthew 26:56; Mark 14:50.
104. Mark 14:51–52.

105. John 18:12-13.
106. John 18:15-18.
107. John 18:19-23.
108. Matthew 26:57; Mark 14:53; Luke 22:54; John 18:24.
109. John 18:14.
110. Matthew 26:57-58; Mark 14:53-54; Luke 22:55.
111. Matthew 26:69-72; Mark 14:66-70; Luke 22:56-58; John 18:25.
112. Matthew 26:73-75; Mark 14:70-72; Luke 22:59-62; John 18:26-27.
113. Luke 22:66.
114. Matthew 26:59-63; Mark 14:55-61.
115. Matthew 26:63-64; Mark 14:61-62; Luke 22:67-70.
116. Matthew 26:65-66; Mark 14:63-64; Luke 22:71.
117. Matthew 27:1; Mark 15:1.
118. Matthew 26:67-68; Mark 14:65; Luke 22:63-65.
119. Isaiah 50:6.
120. Isaiah 52:14.
121. Matthew 27:2; Mark 15:1; Luke 23:1; John 18:28.
122. John 18:29-32. See Matthew 20:18-19.
123. Matthew 27:11; Mark 15:2; Luke 23:2-3; John 18:33-38.
124. John 18:38.
125. Matthew 27:12-14; Mark 15:3-5.
126. Isaiah 53:7.
127. Luke 23:4-5.
128. Luke 23:6-12.
129. Luke 23:13-16.
130. Matthew 27:15-18, 20-23; Mark 15:6-14; Luke 23:17-23; John 18:39-40.
131. Matthew 27:26; Mark 15:15; John 19:1.

132. Psalm 129:3.
133. Matthew 27:27–30; Mark 15:16–19; John 19:2–3.
134. John 19:4–5.
135. John 19:6–11.
136. John 19:12.
137. Matthew 27:19; John 19:13–15.
138. Luke 23:23.
139. Matthew 27:24–26; Mark 15:15; Luke 23:24–25.
140. Matthew 27:26, 31; Mark 15:20; John 19:16.
141. Matthew 27:32–33; Mark 15:21; Luke 23:26, 33; John 19:17.
142. Luke 23:27–31.
143. Luke 23:32.
144. Matthew 27:33–34; Mark 15:22–23; Luke 23:33.
145. Matthew 27:35, 38; Mark 15:25, 27; Luke 23:33; John 19:18.
146. Mark 15:28. See Isaiah 53:12.
147. Psalm 22:16.
148. Mark 15:25.
149. Luke 23:34.
150. Matthew 27:37; Mark 15:26; Luke 23:35–38; John 19:19–22.
151. Psalm 22:18.
152. Matthew 27:35–36; Mark 15:24; Luke 23:34–35; John 19:23–24.
153. Matthew 27:39–44; Mark 15:29–32.
154. John 19:25–27.
155. Luke 23:39–43.
156. Matthew 27:45; Mark 15:33; Luke 23:44–45.
157. Matthew 27:46; Mark 15:34.
158. See Psalm 22:1.

159. Isaiah 53:6; 2 Corinthians 5:21.
160. See Psalm 89:38–45.
161. See Psalm 69:21.
162. Matthew 27:47–49; Mark 15:35–36; John 19:28–29.
163. Matthew 27:50; Mark 15:37; Luke 23:46; John 19:30.
164. 1 Peter 2:24.
165. Isaiah 53:12.
166. Romans 6:23.
167. Hebrews 9:27.
168. Revelation 20:14–15; Revelation 21:8.
169. Romans 5:8.
170. 1 Peter 3:18; Romans 5:10.
171. Isaiah 53:6; Isaiah 53:5.
172. Isaiah 53:10, 12; 1 John 2:2; Romans 6:23.
173. Ephesians 4:9; Matthew 12:40.
174. Psalm 16:10; Acts 2:27.
175. 1 John 4:9–10.
176. Romans 1:16; 1 Corinthians 1:18.
177. 2 Corinthians 9:15.
178. Matthew 12:40, NKJV.
179. Matthew 27:51–52; Mark 15:38; Luke 23:45.
180. Matthew 27:54; Mark 15:39; Luke 23:47.
181. Luke 23:48.
182. Matthew 27:55–56; Mark 15:40–41; Luke 23:49.
183. John 19:31–32.
184. Psalm 34:20.
185. Zechariah 12:10.
186. John 19:33–37.
187. Ephesians 1:7–8.
188. Revelation 1:5.
189. 1 John 1:7.

190. Isaiah 1:18.

191. Psalm 51:7.

192. 1 Corinthians 6:19–20.

193. Matthew 27:3–10; Acts 1:18. See Zechariah 11:12–13.

194. Matthew 27:5; Acts 1:18–19.

195. Matthew 27:57–61; Mark 15:42–47; Luke 23:50–55; John 19:38–42.

196. Matthew 27:62–66.

197. Mark 16:1; Luke 23:56.

198. Ephesians 1:19–20.

199. Acts 2:24.

200. Hebrews 2:14–15.

201. Colossians 2:15.

202. Romans 14:9.

203. Romans 6:4; Romans 4:25; 1 Peter 1:3.

204. Matthew 28:2–4, 11.

205. Matthew 27:52–53.

206. Matthew 28:1; Mark 16:1–4; John 20:1.

207. John 20:2.

208. Matthew 28:5–8; Mark 16:5–8.

209. Matthew 28:11–15.

210. John 20:2.

211. John 20:3–10; Luke 24:12.

212. John 20:11–17.

213. Mark 16:9.

214. Mark 16:10–11; John 20:18.

215. Matthew 28:9–10.

216. Luke 24:1–9.

217. Luke 24:10–11.

218. Luke 24:34.

219. Mark 16:12–13; Luke 24:13–35.

220. Mark 16:14; Luke 24:36–48; John 20:19–23.

221. John 20:24–25.

222. "This book" is a reference to the Gospel of John.

223. John 20:26–31.

224. John 21:1–14.

225. John 21:15–24.

226. Matthew 28:16–17.

227. 1 Corinthians 15:6–7; Acts 1:3.

228. Luke 24:49; Acts 1:2, 5.

229. Matthew 28:18–19; Mark 16:15; Luke 24:46-47.

230. Matthew 28:19-20; Mark 16:15–18.

231. Luke 24:46–47, NKJV.

232. Romans 1:16; 1 Corinthians 1:18.

233. Romans 15:19, NIV, emphasis added.

234. 2 Timothy 4:17, NIV, emphasis added.

235. Galatians 1:6–9 NKJV, emphasis added.

236. See 1 Corinthians 1:17–25.

237. Acts 2:22–41.

238. Acts 3:19, NIV.

239. Acts 3:12–4:4.

240. Acts 4:12, NKJV.

241. Acts 5:30–31, NKJV.

242. 1 Corinthians 1:23–24, NKJV; see also verses 17–25.

243. 1 Corinthians 2:2, NIV; see also verses 1–5.

244. 1 Corinthians 15:1–4, NKJV.

245. Acts 20:20–21, NIV.

246. Galatians 3:1, NKJV.

247. Luke 24:50; Acts 1:6–8, 12.

248. Mark 16:19; Luke 24:50–51; Acts 1:9.

249. Acts 1:10–11.

250. Hebrews 12:2.

251. Ephesians 4:10; Mark 16:19.
252. Hebrews 1:3; Hebrews 2:9.
253. Hebrews 4:14; Hebrews 7:25.
254. Ephesians 4:8, 10.
255. Philippians 2:9–11; Ephesians 1:20–21.
256. Acts 5:31; Acts 2:36.
257. Acts 2:33; Acts 1:4–5, 8.
258. Acts 2:34–35; Psalm 110:1.
259. Ephesians 1:22.
260. 1 Corinthians 15:25–26.
261. Luke 24:52; Acts 1:13.
262. Acts 1:14; Luke 24:53.
263. John 3:16–18.
264. Revelation 3:20.
265. John 1:12–13.
266. Deuteronomy 30:19, NKJV, emphasis added.
267. 1 John 3:23, NIV.
268. Acts 2:38.
269. 2 Peter 3:9, NKJV, emphasis added.
270. John 3:16, NIV.
271. Matthew 18:2–3.
272. Ephesians 2:8–9, NIV, emphasis added.
273. John 1:12–13, NKJV, emphasis added.
274. Revelation 3:20, NKJV, emphasis added.
275. Romans 10:9–10, NIV, emphasis added.
276. See Luke 3:16; Luke 24:49; John 7:37–39; Acts 1:4–5, 8; Acts 2:38–39.
277. Acts 1:8, NIV.
278. 1 John 4:19, NKJV.
279. John 14:15, NIV.
280. Matthew 16:24–25; 2 Corinthians 5:10.

281. 1 Corinthians 6:19–20, NKJV, emphasis added.

282. Acts 1:15–17.

283. Psalm 69:25.

284. Psalm 109:8.

285. Acts 1:20–22.

286. Acts 1:23–26.

287. Acts 2:1–13.

288. Acts 2:14–16.

289. Acts 2:17–21. See Joel 2:28–32.

290. Acts 2:22–25.

291. Acts 2:25–28. See Psalm 16:8–11.

292. Acts 2:29–34.

293. Acts 2:34–35. See Psalm 110:1.

294. Acts 2:36.

295. Acts 2:37–41.

296. Acts 2:42–47.

297. Mark 16:20.